To Cathy:

IF WE KNEW THEN, WHAT WE KNOW NOW

The Power of POSSIBILITIES
for a Longer, Happier, and Healthier Life

By

Allan Katcher, Ph.D.
and
Irving S. Newmark, D.D.S., M.A.
Two Octogenarian Students of Human Behavior

**Copyright © 2011, Allan Katcher, Ph.D.
and Irving S. Newmark, D.D.S., M.A.
Los Angeles, California, U.S.A.**

All rights reserved, including the right to reproduce this book, or any portions thereof, in any form, except for the inclusion of brief quotations in a review, without written permission.

First Printing

Published by CEDEFA

Library of Congress Catalog Number: 2011902803

ISBN: 978-0-9833813-03

Printed in the United States of America

To all our children and grandchildren.
We hope you take full advantage of all the possibilities that
can help you lead a longer, happier and healthier life.

Acknowledgements

The authors are extremely grateful to a number of people who have helped in making this book possible. A primary debt is owed to Gerald Newmark who provided the initial encouragement to write the book and generously provided us permission to use content from his book, *How to Raise Emotionally Healthy Children.*

Dr. Burt Fink, Gloria Katcher, Dr. Dianne Hill, Ken Finn and Sheila Boston have provided time and care to read the book closely, make suggestions about improving the content and style, and add new ideas. We treasure their involvement and are deeply appreciative of their efforts. We also appreciate the invaluable reading and suggestions provided by Mark Rosin.

A special debt is owed to Dr. Philippa Kennealy for her permission to quote from her publication of the Entrepreneurial MD newsletter. Her creative and personal insights add an inspirational quality to the book.

Irv has been a member of a men's group that has been meeting regularly for more than 40 years. Members of this group have shared their lives from death to joy. Much of their wisdom is part of this book. We are deeply grateful for their contributions.

We are deeply grateful to Albert Sarnoff who provided suggestions for editorial changes to make the book more attractive for publication. We also want to express our appreciation to Tuko Fujisaki for her graphics and formatting of the cover material.

Finally, we want to express our gratitude for the wonderful editorial assistance provided by Nancy Marriott who was Dr. Candace Pert's editor for her best-selling *Molecules of Emotion* and Dr. Pert's co-author for *Everything You Need to Know to Feel Go(o)d,* as well as contributing editor for Marci Shimoff's *Happy for No Reason.* Nancy served as a word tunesmith who made our ideas flow.

Table of Contents

IF WE KNEW THEN, WHAT WE KNOW NOW
by

Allan Katcher, Ph.D.

and

Irving S. Newmark, D.D.S., M.A.

Introduction

Have you ever faced a problem so overwhelming that no matter what you did in the face of it, you knew nothing would work? Whatever you could do would cost you pain or money—probably both—and then not even solve the problem. You felt hopelessly trapped, not knowing what to possibly do to make things get any better.

A divorce, a bankruptcy, a hard decision as a parent—these are just some of the difficulties life throws at us. Most people have experienced such distress or the equivalent at least once in their lives, if not many times. If you have undergone such difficult times, you know what it's like to look down a long, dark tunnel and see no light of hope at the end.

We two octogenarians, Allan and Irving, have certainly had our own tough times and in the course of our lives made many mistakes. But we've learned a simple yet profound lesson: *There are always more ways to think about a problem than might be apparent at the time.*

In our lives, we have found that the hardest thing to do—but the most rewarding—was to look for and choose new possibilities for dealing with situations that at the time seemed totally hopeless. The popular quote from Shakespeare, "There are more things in life than you or I have imagined, Horatio," sums it up, as does the familiar adage, *There are more ways than one to skin a cat.*

And indeed, there are.

In this book, you will start to see the many possibilities that are available to solve your most challenging problems and realize you are not as trapped as you may feel. You will be encouraged to examine your feelings and perspectives on major issues in life, and to take one step beyond your current view to see solutions you couldn't see before. When you look at your particular situation from a different perspective, a solution that seemed strange or unfamiliar before can become exactly what you need to provide the outcome you want.

Who We Are

Meeting for breakfasts and lunches over many years, we two have shared our experiences, exchanged stories about the people in our lives, and thought about what could be different. Out of those meetings came some simple wisdom, and so we decided to share that wisdom by writing this book.

Allow us to introduce ourselves:

Irv has been practicing dentistry for over 60 years and has lectured extensively on doctor-patient relationships. He obtained a degree in psychology, and co-authored a book with his brother Gerald entitled, *Happiness Through Superficiality: The War Against Meaningful Relationships*. In 1956, he founded the Studio City Dental Group, the longest running group in the United States. This group is his ongoing laboratory to explore and handle the many problems with patient care, including relationships between colleagues, patient fears and concerns. (I know intimately about the quality of care provided by Irv's office, because I, Allan, am one of his patients.)

Allan began his career as a professor at the University of Washington, teaching courses in child psychology, social psychology and personality. Later he was a co-developer of the Life Orientations Training (LIFO®) Method, a system for identifying personal and managerial styles that has been taught to more than 8 million people worldwide. He has published three books: *The Importance of Being Yourself*, *Managing Your Strengths* and *Learning Dynamics*. At the University of Washington, he also taught a course on doctor-patient relationships and has traveled the world lecturing about interpersonal relationships in 26 countries.

The origins of our friendship stem from a mutual interest in management and psychology. We met through Irv's brother Jerry who shared a commuter ride with Allan, going daily from the San Fernando Valley to Santa Monica, California, for work at the System Development Corporation. Jerry mentioned his brother taught courses to dentists on how to manage their relationships with patients and invited me (Allan) to meet Irv and sit in on one of his sessions. I accepted and as a result became utterly fascinated by what Irv was doing. I observed the involvement and interest he created in his audience, and even more than that, I saw how he provided a framework that was highly meaningful to everyone. After more meetings, we got together and decided to design a course for UCLA's Extension Division that would focus on helping dentists manage their practice and patient relationships.

Our business relationship turned into friendship based on being students of human behavior. We realized we'd learned and experienced much in our 169 combined years of living. Getting together and looking back over our own lives, we often asked the question, *If we knew then, what we know now, could we have been healthier and happier?* The answers that came up during the course of those conversations led to much discussion of creative solutions to problems we'd dealt with and people are dealing with now, and we decided that a book with such a focus would be meaningful for others.

If you have ever done a similar review of your life, you might very well come to the same conclusions we did. There is wisdom in experience, and one person's hindsight can be another's foresight. Hopefully, you will discover your own wisdom in reading this book, and along the way gain strategies for healthier and happier living.

● ● ● ● ● ● ● ●

As you read *If We Knew Then, What We Know Now*, you will find many stories of experiences that sound familiar, along with some guidelines that suggest doing things differently than you are prone to do now. These guidelines suggest ways to minimize your stress and provide more lasting satisfaction in life. They will enable you to maintain your integrity, yet look at issues with more objectivity. Each chapter in Part II on five key areas of life—intimate relationships, parenting, financial security, work and health—poses provocative questions about your behavior and attitudes. Presented at the beginning of the chapter, these questions are aimed at cultivating self-awareness and self-examination, and you will find value in answering them before proceeding to read the chapter.

In your reading, you will learn how you block yourself from being able to see opportunities that exist and could solve your problems. You will be asked to look at the subsequent distress that often has negative impact on your health and other areas of your life. You will also be given a vision of a world full of possibilities awaiting your choice if you are flexible enough to make use of those possibilities. It is our hope that you are willing to try some new behaviors, to learn and change, so you can experience less distress and more happiness and health in your life.

Explore the Possibilities!

Part I
Basic Concepts

Chapter 1
The Power of Possibilities

In reviewing our own lives, what stood out as a major blind spot for both of us was the failure to make use of possibilities that were available but at the time hidden from our view. We had travelled through life making choices based on what we already knew, when so many alternate paths we did not choose could have taken us in more beneficial directions.

Perhaps you recall the lines from Robert Frost's poem, *The Road Not Taken,* in which the poet describes two paths encountered in life. "I took the road less traveled by, and that made all the difference," Frost writes about coming to a major crossroad in his life and choosing the less familiar path. So often, we feel compelled to act or to do what we've always done and found useful—the more traveled road—not realizing there was another and even possibly better way to respond.

If you look, you, too, may be able to see another way, a road less traveled for resolving issues you are facing in your marriage, your family, or your business. Consider the following examples: A couple constantly fought about tidiness in their home, their feelings escalating into a full-blown battle. Hiring a maid to clean up once a week was an obvious but long overlooked solution. Another couple believed they shouldn't ever go into debt and were deeply depressed when they experienced a number of financial hardships. Nevertheless, there were other possibilities available to alleviate their situation, such as reducing their expenses or one or both getting another job, to mention just a few.

Even when things look their worst, it can pay to look outside of your current circumstances for a new approach or new solution to ongoing difficulties. How do you do this? Start by asking others to share suggestions and then try some different paths than the one you have been on. Simply you changing course and trying something new can powerfully alter a situation to change your life. This is what Frost was pointing to, and what we are calling the *power of possibilities.*

Recently, we were talking with a group of people about the power of possibilities, when a man in the audience angrily interrupted our talk. "It's nice to talk about considering the possibilities," he said, obviously frustrated, "but I'm financially strapped right now. I have an 18-year-old kid who is rebellious, and a wife who is rarely sympathetic and always critical. I'm up against a wall, so where do I find any possibilities for the problems in my life?"

We had to admit he had a point. It's certainly easier to look at and find possibilities when you're not experiencing such severe problems. You may remember however, those times when you were discussing important issues with friends, and someone suggested a solution or idea that you never could have thought of yourself. An important source of new possibilities is the suggestions of friends, especially those who don't know you so well that they might become blindsided by all they know about you and your situation.

At times, professionals can also provide additional ideas to explore. In the case of the angry man in our audience, there was much in his life to explore with a therapist or counselor. In looking deeper, he might find that his son needs to feel loved by his parents, his wife is critical because she is anxious and frustrated by how he handles money, and his habits are causing him to assume debts he can't afford. Once these factors are explored, he might see opportunities he didn't see before, for example, selling some assets or finding a better-paying job. So often, problems in life obscure the solutions, having us focus on the hard times and miss the possibilities that were and are always there.

Evaluating New Possibilities

Suggestions from friends and experts can be helpful, but you may feel so overwhelmed by the issues you're facing, you don't know where to start. Here are a few simple steps you can take to begin to find and evaluate new possibilities for situations that concern you.

1. **Explore possibilities without any judgment**. You may be in the habit of classifying possible solutions as to their value, saying to yourself: *This is a good one, this one isn't*. But before you divide up and eliminate any choices, simply explore your options without judgment during this phase. Make a list of all the possibilities that come to mind without evaluating any of them until after you've completed your list.

2. **Assign probability.** Once you've made your list, look to see which possibilities have a high probability of working and

eliminate those that don't. You probably know at least one person who always thinks of what will go wrong when contemplating new ideas and therefore never takes a step. Avoid this by looking clearly at what is most probably going to solve the problem and being realistic. Even though a lot of your possibilities have very little chance of happening, it doesn't mean you should never choose them

3. **Evaluate the possibility.** How will you know if a particular possibility on your list will work? In the case of the couple mentioned above who felt they should never go into debt, they might ask: *Will getting a different job provide more income, reduce debt, or relieve our anxieties?* Each life situation requires a different answer, so you want to have specific criterion against which the possibility you are considering can be evaluated for its potential to help you achieve your goal.

4. **Consider the action, not just the idea of the possibility.** *Synectics*, a problem-solving system for encouraging creativity in the workplace, emphasizes the importance of giving full consideration to what might be needed to make a particular possibility work. Researchers developing Synectics found that groups too often rejected solutions, because people only looked at the first expression of an idea rather than at the actions steps necessary to make that idea work. Think through the steps you would take in exploring a new possibility. For the debt-avoiding couple, this might entail the actual steps involved in seeking new employment for one or both of them.

The Value of Self-Awareness

The value of self-awareness and self-review is critical for emotional health and happiness. Without carefully examining your life and how you are living it, you won't be able to make wise choices and take advantage of possibilities when times are tough. Unfortunately, you—like most of us—probably tend to look at your behavior more often *after* the fact than before it, which is why we have provided frameworks and methods for doing life review throughout this book. Looking at mistakes made in the past is never an easy process, but it can help you plan ahead for more satisfaction in the future.

Awareness can help you in every area of life. Dr. Dean Ornish, in an exciting book called *The Spectrum*, points out how awareness fosters health. *Awareness is the first step in healing. When we become more aware of how powerfully our choices in diet and lifestyle affect us—for better and for worse—then we can make different ones. It's like connecting the dots. In our experience, many people are not afraid to make big changes in their lives if they understand the benefits of doing so and how quickly they may occur.*

In this book, we will be encouraging you to examine your life, so you can become aware of the choices you are making. In addition, we also want you to realize that there are usually more possibilities to choose from than you have imagined. It is our goal to help you discover what those possibilities might be and take advantage of the opportunities they offer, especially when you are under stress and unhappy in your life.

There are many reasons why people don't examine their lives.

Sometimes, we "know" too much. The word *know* is in quotes, because what we think we know may not be the same as actually knowing it. An example of this comes directly out of Allan's life.

Many years ago, Allan bought a sail boat and decided he ought to learn how to sail. In typically academic fashion, he hired an instructor and proceeded to read a slew of books on sailing. During the first lesson, the instructor suggested many things to do, but Allan replied, "That's not what the book said!" After several rounds of this, the instructor shouted angrily, "You know more than you understand!" Only then, could the learning begin.

It was as if Allan were trying to use book knowledge as a substitute for experience. You, too, may sometimes think you know all about a subject and therefore are unwilling to listen to information or suggestions from others. Until *what you know* becomes an integral part of *what you do*, it is only empty learning. It is too easy to pretend you know, but not truly understand, and therefore not look deeply enough at your life and question your behavior and motives.

The Willingness to Be Responsible

Something else we have learned in our 169 combined years of living and growing is that insight alone is not enough to make a change. In Phillip Roth's book, *Portnoy's Complaint*, after endless discussion of everything Portnoy has found painful, he says to his therapist, "I suppose I might have had something to do with all that." The therapist replies, "And now we begin!" It wasn't only Portnoy's insight that caused his therapist's reply, but Portnoy's apparent willingness to take responsibility for his life that provoked the comment.

For all of us, change begins when we become aware that we are responsible for the choices we make in life. For you to change your circumstances, you will have to acknowledge your responsibility, commit to new behaviors, and practice those behaviors to make them your new habits for dealing with old situations. This means you have to be aware of what you do and why you do it, catching yourself in the act, so to speak, and then doing something different.

Any change you create needs to be measured by the effect it is having on others. If you think you have changed and others don't notice it, you have to ask why. Have you alerted others to the fact you're trying to change? Are you using new behaviors, and if so, how well are you using them? Have you asked for feedback about this, so the changes you are making can be confirmed by others?

Why Don't We Do What Makes Sense?

Old habits die hard, even with responsibility and awareness. Why do we create such dilemmas and pain in making decisions when we don't have to? If we deliberately tried to design events to happen badly, we probably couldn't come close to achieving what actually happens.

Look around you and see how many differences there are between people that develop into habitual patterns of behavior and relationship, even when those patterns are not productive. For example, some people are cautious and deliberate, and have difficulty responding to rapid changes. Others charge quickly into battle to begin verbal sparring when softer words would achieve a better effect.

Such habitual behaviors, often derived from successful experiences and models, can become automatic ways of behaving. On the one hand, these strategies offer simple and comfortable ways of coping, but when overdone they may become self-defeating.

We all face many dilemmas when it comes to responding to life. It's one thing to be generous but another to be an easy mark for anyone who requests a handout. It's great to respond rapidly to crises, but awful if you're so impulsive you make costly errors. Being thoughtful and deliberate, and pondering many aspects of an issue may make for good decisions, but if the deliberations take too long, you can become overwhelmed by events. It's one thing to be bold but another to deliberately put yourself, your fortune, and your family in danger by taking huge risks. We will discuss such dilemmas in depth in later chapters.

Additional Value of Knowing Yourself

Only when you know yourself deeply and are fully aware of the consequences of your unproductive behaviors, can you maintain control over events to gain maximum satisfaction and security. A key self-discovery is learning when *more* is too much, and *less* is not enough. Learning this takes experience and making a commitment to examine yourself and your behaviors, especially those that have become ingrained patterns.

If you're lucky and have people in your life who can listen attentively and that you trust, then ask for some honest feedback to help you see what's happening in a particular situation that concerns you. It's never easy to receive feedback, and everyone tends to put on their defensive hat before being willing to hear the truth. But if you consider what's being said over time, without rejecting it outright, you may see some light and make some new choices.

Knowing yourself means you can trust your intuition and go with your gut feelings when it comes to making decisions. When you feel good about what is happening or will happen, you're probably making the right decision. When you're uptight and tense, and feel uncomfortable about something you're doing or have to do, it's probably not the wisest thing to do. Even so, there will be times when you want to be spontaneous, to be free to act at the moment, but remember to always look at the consequences your choice will engender. Evaluate the impact your actions may have on those closest to you, your career, your friends and colleagues. See if what you are choosing is worth the price you may have to pay.

Reviewing Your Life: A Journal Exercise

To gain a new perspective and possibly choose a different path, take a moment and review the meaning and significance of your life. Like us, you may have found that in living, you have learned some things that are profound and worth passing on. If so, consider that you have the opportunity to do that right now. It doesn't matter how old you are, only that you are willing to see your life objectively.

The following exercise is meant to be done by writing in a journal, so take out a notebook and find a quiet place to contemplate your answers to record before you move on in this book. Keep your journal in a safe place so you can return to it at the end of the book and see if you would change or write differently any answers that occur to you now.

1. What do you view as your accomplishments that were significant and worthwhile?
2. Of all those, which one is the most important to you?
3. What do you feel you have given to those you love?
4. What have you learned that you would want to leave as wisdom for others?
5. What do you wish you could have done with your life that you didn't do?
6. What words would you leave for those who are most important to you?

Doing such a review of your life is not an easy task. You may find that there is nothing you can write, in which case, take more time to contemplate your possible answers, returning to the job at a later time. You may have some regrets about what you haven't been able to do. This is all part of the value of the exercise, which is to have you think about what has happened—and what you want to happen—in your life.

Once you have brought your awareness to this critical process of self-examination and review, you will find you are able to see what is unfamiliar—the road less traveled—and begin to take advantage of the power of possibilities, now and in the future.

• • • • • • • •

Throughout the next chapters in this book, we will explore attitudes and behaviors in every area of your life to help you make the words you wrote in the above exercise come to life. Read the sections that seem appropriate and relevant for you, or read all of the sections in order—it doesn't matter. But we recommend that you don't skip the next chapter on emotional health, because you being able to understand emotions—how they can help you and hurt you—is key to you envisioning a different future and having happiness and health in every area of your life.

Chapter 2
Emotional Health—What It *Is*, and What It *Isn't*

Emotional health is fundamental in your ability to see and use possibilities for resolving issues in your life. When you have emotional health, you can see solutions that may already exist and that you might otherwise miss. Then, life becomes an adventure of *what's next*, rather than a journey over rough road to a dead end, leaving you feeling hopeless and trapped with nowhere to turn.

An Emotionally Healthy Life

Your behavior directly relates to your emotional health, so it is useful to look at different ways of living that can be characterized as *emotionally healthy*. This is not to say that there is an absolute state of emotional health, but there are times when what you are doing makes for healthy living, and times that it does not.

We use the term *emotional health* to mean living in such a way that you are relatively free of distress, while at the same time you have an awareness and understanding of yourself. Emotionally healthy people are comfortable with intimacy, have a practical grasp of reality, are willing to learn, and are able to make choices that result in their satisfaction without causing harm to others.

Simply put, if you are emotionally healthy, you will find more meaning and significance in what you do and feel happier about your life than others who are not. This doesn't imply that emotional health is always free of distress, fear, pain, and dilemmas, but if you are emotionally healthy, these factors will not dominate your life in a persistent way.

In Part II of this book, we will examine issues that commonly arise in each of five important areas of life and see how those issues can be responded to in emotionally healthy or unhealthy ways. We will suggest paths that are more consistent with principles of emotional health. A breakdown in one or more of the five areas can cause significantly negative emotional and/or physical health problems. We also think it is important for you to become aware of how your current behavior in each life area either satisfies your basic psychological needs or does not, another measure of emotional health.

Understanding Emotional Health

A common misunderstanding about emotional health is that you should not be emotional. Showing your emotions has somehow come to mean you are weak or out of control, and therefore not healthy. On the contrary, emotionally healthy people experience their emotions and feelings fully, and are free to express them. The difference is they don't let their emotions govern their behavior without consideration of the consequences.

We learn early to suppress our emotions. It may be that in your childhood, you were not encouraged by your parents to express certain emotions, such as fear or anger, or even love. If this suppressive attitude was accompanied by intense punishment or terrifying events, you may not be aware of your emotions when they occur in adulthood, and so are more likely to be influenced by them because they are not under your control.

As you mature, learning and cultural pressures encourage you to consider the consequences, modify your behavior with age, and become aware of your emotions while controlling their expressions. This is all very good, but your experience of your emotions is important for you to understand, so you can make choices in what you *want* to do, as compared with what you think you *should* do. In any kind of intimate relationship, for example, it is important that you are able to express emotions and empathize with those who you are closest to.

However, it is natural that extremely intense emotions occur more often when you feel frustrated, deeply disappointed, attacked or misunderstood, especially by an intimate partner. As you mature, you learn to not make crucial decisions based on your emotions. If you are angry with your children, you know it is not wise to cut off their inheritance or threaten them with bodily harm.

An emotion is neither bad nor good—it simply *is*, a part of your natural being. In emotionally healthy living, you are aware of your emotions—the capacity to feel love, anger, joy, despair, grief, excitement, the full range of possible feelings—and you accept them for what they are.

Too often, because of your own experience of being suppressed as a child, you respond to the emotions of others negatively: *Don't feel angry! You shouldn't feel that way! Good girls wouldn't feel sorry, Boys aren't afraid of such things!* These expressions are neither psychologically helpful nor conducive to emotional health. The person with those feelings *does* feel that way—and you must try to understand why.

Often when people perceive you are making a sincere attempt to understand them, they become less intense in their expression and may even try to help you by explaining their feelings more clearly. However, neither they nor you can always understand why a particular emotion is being experienced, because the reason may be unconscious. If negative feelings are repetitive, obsessive, or overly dominating in your behavior, and you don't know why, you may want to seek professional help to understand the meaning of the emotion resulting in your behavior.

Basic Needs and Emotional Health

A list of basic human needs can be endless, varying hugely from person to person, but there are some basic needs that must be met for you to maintain emotional health. Five of the most important basic needs have been identified by Gerald Newmark in his book, *How to Raise Emotionally Healthy Children.* They are:

- The need to feel respected
- The need to feel important
- The need to feel accepted
- The need to feel included
- The need to feel secure

In each of the five life areas we cover in Part II, we will look at how our behaviors satisfy these basic needs, and thus help us to be emotionally healthy and open to life's many possibilities.

Unconscious Factors in Emotional Health

You may feel that the process of examination we are emphasizing is too rational for evaluating your behavior and the reactions of others to it. In part, that is true, and we don't mean to underplay the influence of spontaneous and unconscious forces, which must also be considered. Nevertheless, the act of examining your behavior begins to help you make sense of some troubling and confusing situations you find yourself in.

Certainly there are unconscious forces that influence your behavior and lead you to act in ways that seem irrational and non-functional. We know of one situation where a reasonably contented husband was driven to have affairs, even though he regretted his behavior and experienced deep guilt about it. It seemed as if he were addicted to such behavior and could not understand it rationally. In such cases, logic alone may not yield the reason for a behavior, and the skilled services of a psychotherapist are required to understand why such behavior is happening.

In fact, your choice of an intimate partner may be highly unconscious, despite recognition of the virtues of the loved person. Perhaps there are similarities—both *pro* and *con*—between your intended spouse and a parent, depending on early parental experiences. Perhaps a disruption in your marriage is due to your spouse having been influenced by being a member of a dysfunctional family as a child. To some extent, many of your of choices and behaviors are powerfully influenced by unconscious factors, and you may not be aware of them at the time.

Cultural Factors and Emotional Health

Unconscious forces that shape emotional health can be cultural, social and even familial.

Each of us is exposed to a normative pattern of attitudes and behaviors embedded in our particular culture of origin and social class that influences us on an unconscious level. In the United States, there are expectations about legal resolutions of differences that are not the same as expectations in many Latin American countries. If you are a member of the middle class in some countries, there are codes for social behavior that differ from those of lower- and upper-class members.

In multinational companies, where two different cultures come together, differences can create barriers, misunderstanding, and even hostilities. A Japanese manager may find American employees too undisciplined, while an American manager might regard Japanese employees as too rigid and bureaucratic. It takes time to translate what is expected behavior for one culture into the psychological framework of another before good teamwork can occur.

A company's social culture can vary according to the values held by the people running the organization and have profoundly different impacts. In one major aircraft company, a heavily bureaucratic culture emphasized the power of certain positions and forms of communication, severely punishing anyone for spontaneous and unasked for opinions. Google's culture, in contrast, is famous for its openness, informal clothing, open lines of communication, limited bureaucracy, and encouragement of innovative thoughts and opinions.

Even from family to family, there are cultural influences. One family believes in the open expression of feelings, such as affection and admiration, as well as respect for individual boundaries. Another family may have emphasized control of feelings and caution in revealing feelings to non-family members, even showing little open affection to each other. Familial patterns tend to be repetitive and heavily reinforced, with the expectation of general conformity to the espoused values. You may behave automatically when within a culture because of this, but be unaware of the behavioral and attitudinal preferences that you possess.

Sometimes strong cultural differences are experienced within a marriage and pose difficulties in understanding and relating. This is often the case when partners come from different cultural backgrounds. For example, if one partner is more Italian, accustomed to outbursts of emotional passion, and another is more British, preferring contained restraint, they might easily misunderstand each other. What one partner would see as a normal and vital life expression of anger might be perceived by the other as threatening or madness. On the other hand, the quiet behavior of the British partner might be seen by an Italian as boring and passive. Of course, in intimate relationships, romance may cause you to overlook these differences at first, sometimes with resulting disappointment.

In a parody of national cultural differences, the inscription on a mock award trophy belonging to Allan reads: *The perfect European should be as humorous as a German, as patient as an Austrian, as available as a Russian, as generous as a Dutchman, as controlled as an Italian, as flexible as a Swede, as talkative as a Finn, as humble as a Spaniard, as sober as the Irish, as organized as a Greek.*

Jim Cramer, the host of the TV program *Mad Money*, emphasizes the importance of doing your homework before investing money. The same is true for relationships. When you take the time to understand cultural differences between you and a partner, you're more likely to value and enjoy those differences—a sure sign of emotional health.

Basic Guidelines for Emotional Health

Before we continue to discuss how emotional health can impact issues in your life, we want to list some principles that have been helpful to us in our lives to ensure emotional health. Sometimes we've found that it's necessary to stop and take stock of what is happening before reacting, otherwise the consequences may be too severe. We found that when we failed to follow these guidelines, we got into trouble and unnecessarily so.

We hope these basic guidelines will help you to achieve emotionally healthy behavior in all of the areas that are discussed, and provide some guidance when you're caught in a conflict or have to make an important decision. The directions may sound simple, but they're often difficult to follow if you allow yourself to be carried away by your feelings. Hopefully, you will find them all as meaningful and useful as we have.

1. **Give a little to get a lot.** Carefully measure what you are doing and give in on little things to prevent major problems.

You may get what you want immediately, but is it worth the price you will have to pay? Sometimes it pays to sacrifice what you want now in order to achieve your long term goal.

2. **Pay only once, not twice or more.** This applies to financial issues, but also to emotional issues. Think of all the guilt (emotional price) you suffer after an error or argument occurs. Don't keep refreshing that bad feeling by wallowing in regret. When it's over, it's over. Otherwise, you're going to stay stuck and likely cause more of the same feelings.

3. **Get it out of the way.** When there is a distasteful task, do it first or set aside a time to do it. Get it out of the way. If you don't, it will be in your head until it's done, taking up valuable space otherwise available to enjoy new adventures and come up with new possibilities.

4. **Let it lie.** Not everything your significant other says needs a response. Consider how the other person is feeling: He or she experiences anger, but it could have nothing to do with you. Rather, it's simply their own experience.

5. **Stay off the defensive.** An apparent attack may vanish when there is little or no response by you. Try to restrain yourself from counter-attacking, even though you may not be able to help feeling defensive. The other person may be simply trying to tell you how intensely he or she is feeling, not attacking you or looking for a fight. Sometimes the person's reaction to advice may be an immediate defense against feeling blamed. Yet, when there has been time for later thought, the person

may have a change of mind leading to acceptance of that advice.

6. **Give advice only when called for.** Check first before offering any kind of advice or suggestion. If you have something important to say, you might ask the other person if he or she would be interested in another viewpoint. This is not an absolute dictum. In many cases the failure to give advice can be taken as disinterest—as in the case of a child hoping to get advice from a parent. However, don't be surprised if your advice gets rejected or is treated with anger, because it wasn't requested or welcomed.

7. **Have a goal in choosing your action.** *If you don't know where you're going, any road will get you there,* said the Cheshire Cat in *Alice in Wonderland.* For emotional health, this translates to knowing what you want from an encounter or situation before allowing it to happen. Consider carefully the consequences of decisions you wish to make and the possible feelings they may incite. On the other hand, you don't want to squelch all spontaneity, so strive for a balance.

8. **Go for what works.** Sometimes, a choice that seems impossible and has little chance of gaining agreement may be the most appropriate course of action. When considering what may "work," ask what the consequence will be, both in the short and long term.

9. **Don't talk it to death.** When your point is accepted and you have agreement, stop talking and acknowledge the other per-

son's assent. Too often good ideas get trampled in the process, because one or the other partner wants to be seen as "right."

10. **Be yourself and allow others the same.** Mutual respect and acknowledgment of differences lets you know that what you are asking may not fit the other person, so compromises and/or tradeoffs should be sought, rather than waging a war of differences.

11. **Be willing to relinquish feeling good to get at the truth**. It is important for you to keep in mind that your feelings and beliefs, while true to yourself, may be limited and even blind. Try to experience what people are trying to tell you about their feelings and beliefs, so you can find a *win-win* solution in which both parties gain something valuable out of the encounter.

12. **Don't let money be a problem.** If a problem can be solved with money, it isn't really a problem. (This is assuming you have the money or have access to it.) Such a situation can arise because you don't want to spend money, not because spending money will seriously deplete your resources. If the physical and psychological health of a loved one is at stake, there should be little hesitancy in making money available to that person. However, be aware that while providing money can solve an immediate problem, it can also enable irresponsibility and dependence.

We thought our list of basic emotional needs was complete until we read an article in a newsletter published by our friend, Dr. Philippa Kennealy. Dr. Kennealy, who has a website called The Entrepreneurial MD, wrote a list that seemed so meaningful, we asked her permission to reproduce it here for you:

Five Truths to Tide You Over When the Well Appears Dry

Despite the oft repeated idea that healthcare is recession-proof, many of the physicians I've spoken to in recent months have reported drops in patient attendance, a fall-off in clientele in their businesses, and declining incomes. Politics and reimbursements aside, it's apparent that even an essential like medical care has taken a hit in the recession.

This drying up of the pipeline (sorry – maybe an oil metaphor is a poor choice now; I'm thinking of it more as a water pipeline!) is scary, as there is no end in sight. It introduces uncertainty, which we tolerate poorly.

My trip to Africa sparked once again my awareness that, as bad as we think we have it, there are those for whom a dry bed in a rain storm, because the corrugated iron roof isn't leaking, is a blessing. And a discarded pair of still-clean but slightly worn running shoes is a veritable luxury. I returned to the U.S., fortified by these five truths that remind me that, barring any personal or family tragedy, I am going to be okay.

1. Your happiness is directly proportional to your resilience.

Earlier, I mentioned the pioneering spirit I re-encountered in South Africa, and even more so in Zimbabwe. It is almost inconceivable that I still have very dear friends living in a country that has been so trashed by its leadership that it is almost unrecognizable. And yet there they are, willing to share a laugh over a beer around a fire in the evening, making shopping lists for the next trip into town, and coping with ticks, malaria and outrageous food prices! This is hardy stock. And I know that deep down inside, I am hardy stock, too. Just as you are when it's called for

2. Your skills and training will ALWAYS find use somewhere.

Hate your practice because of whiny patients or poor pay? Frantic to quit as you know you can't do this forever, but terrified that you'll never get something else going for you? What if I reassured you that you would never *really* fall on your face? Not with all that marvelous training and experience. Not if you were willing to shed some of the padding from your life and give yourself the fall-back option of practicing medicine in other countries where a) you would be ever so appreciated, b) the costs of living as translated into US dollars would be much lower and c) you could feel like you were making a huge difference. Would you take the plunge and get something else going (even if it meant keeping your detested job for now).

3. Your needs are far simpler than you imagine.

As soon as I get away from Los Angeles and into a less privileged area, I am struck by how much less I really need. I could sell three quarters of my wardrobe and still be fine. I could donate half of my kitchen ware and still produce a decent meal. My travels to Italy, France, China and Africa have shown me that people all over the world, living civilized and purposeful lives, manage with way less than I have. I know I could do it. What about you?

4. Your fears are almost always fictitious.

Srikumar Rao reminded us of this fact in our March teleclass: We invent most of our fears, especially those that interfere with our sleep. Sure there is stuff to be scared of – bad guys, car accidents, unbearable losses. But unless they are happening to you right now, any thoughts about these and other dire situations are future speculations or past recollections. Pain is awful when you have it, whether it is physical or psychological, and I would never want to gloss over that.

However, most of our pain is self-created and originates in fear (or False Evidence Appearing Real). Stop right now and check yourself for the signs and symptoms of *present* physical or emotional pain. If it's there, nurture yourself and do what you must to take care of yourself. If you don't discover any, then know that you are okay right now, *despite* your fear.

5. Your "You" is inviolable.

This is the biggest truth for me. This is the time I resort to my thoughts about those who made it through the Holocaust. No matter how degrading their circumstances, no matter how much brutality they faced, no matter the sheer horror of their day-to-day existence, survivors like Eli Wiesel failed to relinquish their "You"–their souls. This attitude represents the ultimate in courage. I believe I could show courage if I truly needed to. Bet you would, too!

I offer you these personal reminders from my African escapade in the spirit of hope and faith that you too have answers. If your well is looking dry at present and you have a gnawing anxiety about the future, please pause for a moment and examine yourself to discover your own truths. Can you adapt to challenging circumstances if you have to? Will you ultimately be okay, deep down inside? And if you knew you would and could, what permission do you need to give yourself to tolerate the current drought or, better still, to blaze new trails or undertake future adventures?

• • • • • • • •

Rate Yourself

Before you begin Part II, rate your level of success in each of the key areas of life below on a scale of 1 to 10. A rating of 10 represents the maximum possible success or desirable state, and a rating of 1 represents the least.

___Intimate Relationship
___Parenting
___Financial Security
___Work
___Health

As you read the material in Part II about these five areas, you may find it useful to imagine how your scores would change if you changed certain aspects of your behavior. Making significant changes in any of those five areas can give you access to seeing and choosing new possibilities in your life that are always available to you.

Part II
Five Key Areas of Life

Chapter 3
Intimate Relationships

Your intimate relationships—whether you are in a marriage or a long-term commitment—can give you the most satisfaction and fulfillment in life, and also the most anguish and despair. This is because every aspect of your life is impacted by the happiness in your intimate relationship, or lack of it. In this chapter, we will deal with the elements of intimate relationships that are so basic and fundamental, they underlie all other life areas examined in this book.

A Personal Assessment

Before reading further, take this personal assessment to examine your current relationship. (If you are not currently in a relationship, use your last relationship as an example.) When you finish reading the chapter, do another assessment using the same questions, imagining this time that you and your partner have made use of the material and changed your behavior to provide more emotional health in your partnership.

Ask yourself the following questions and write your answers here or in your journal:

1. What would you describe as the strengths of your relationship?

   _____

   _____

2. What do you see as each partner's strengths?

   _____

   _____

3. How are those strengths being used in the relationship?

   _____

   _____

4. What areas of your relationship do you feel need to be improved?

   _____

   _____

5. What's the one thing that bugs you most about your relationship?

   _____

   _____

On a scale of 1-10, 10 being high and 1 low, rate your satisfaction with your relationship and write that rating in your journal or here for future comparison. _____

Choosing an Intimate Partner

At one point, you chose the intimate relationship you are now in. What were you looking for at that time? There are countless possibilities of relationships to choose from when deciding to enter a life partnership. You may have hoped for a passionate, intense, caring and sharing relationship full of activity and drama. Another possibility is a relationship that is calm, peaceful, companionable and controlled. A third could alternate between being both close and distant, changing constantly, yet full of care. A less desirable possibility might be one that is full of conflict, angry shouting, possessiveness and jealousy with occasional peaks of joyous sharing.

Which possibility of a relationship did you seek? What are you experiencing in that relationship now? What would you like to be experiencing? These are all good questions to have in mind as we take a look at how the relationship you are now in began.

Looking back, it may be hard to remember why you chose your intimate partner. In interviews, people offer a variety of reasons for choosing their partners:

- "She was absolutely gorgeous. When I saw her, I knew I had to get to know her."
- "He looked so solid and strong, as if you would always feel protected by him."
- "She was sitting by herself at a dance, and I went over to talk to her. She replied warmly, and we started talking about all kinds of things. I felt she would be an ideal companion."
- "I liked his sensitivity and warmth – he seemed to deal easily with everyone. I don't know what it was, but we hit it off right away. We laughed at the same things, had similar interests and had fun in whatever we did."
- "I loved his eyes – it seemed like he could see right through me and know me instantly without judgment."
- "He was so sexy and a wonderful lover!"
- "She looked like the woman I could take home to the family, and

she would fit right in."

It might have been looks, attitude and manner, joyous enthusiasm, seriousness about life issues, a caring manner, intellectual interests or something else. Your choice may have been validated by experience, or you may have found the choice didn't pan out the way you hoped. The basis for choice, however, has been found to be a primary factor in the success of relationships.

When things go awry in your relationship, think back to why you were attracted to your partner in the first place, and it may help you find another way of thinking about the troubling issues. For example, knowing your partner is a very sensitive and caring person, you can understand her anger was because you behaved in a critical and unfeeling manner many times in the past, rather than because of something specific you were doing now.

Choosing a mate is such a problem, however. You're bombarded by the fiction of love, the primacy of passion, and the fantasies of everlasting tenderness and affection. Your wishes are likely to be so intense that they often overpower your thinking, and you deny all that could be seen if your eyes were truly open. This happens to even the most experienced and sophisticated people. No one is immune.

A colleague, an expert in predicting compatibility, gave his prospective mate a series of tests to enlighten both as to their possibilities for getting along. The tests clearly identified major sources of incompatibility, yet the colleague went ahead with the marriage. Years later, when undergoing therapy, he was asked how he could have made such a choice in light of his knowledge. His reply was, "She was so beautiful!" Blinded, he had failed to notice how irascible and violent she could be in quarrels and disagreements. You may have had similar kinds of disenchanting experiences because of factors in a relationship that you had overlooked.

When you step back and think of a long term commitment, you can see that you need to have more than the initial attraction to make the relationship work. Maybe you could have made a better choice if you had the experience of living together before becoming intimate partners. While some couples may live together many years, it may not guarantee emotionally healthy relationships. However, getting married after taking time to know each other well is helpful. Unfortunately, cultural or family pressures may not support such a practice.

The future son-in-law of a friend of ours asked for an audience with our friend and his wife, explaining that he wanted to ask for their daughter's hand in marriage. The father said they would be happy to say yes, providing the young man and their daughter first answered some questions. He wanted to see if the two knew each other well enough to get married. However, from the young man's answers, it was apparent they did not. The parents then suggested the two of them live together for awhile instead of getting married. The young petitioner said, "But I respect your daughter! We need to get married!" Our friend replied, "You ought to first find out who it is you intend to marry!"

Think back to your own family experiences. You may have grown up in a family that provided instances of caring and involvement, as well as conflicts and bitterness. You knew that sometimes your parents were deeply troubled by their differences and other times experienced joy when things went well. You may have observed that your parents were overly critical, and you were hurt by their remarks, or seen that caring statements made pains dissolve. Some parents were interested in what was happening in each other's day, while others could care less. In short, you have had experiences that could be the basis for your choice. Therefore, a valuable source of information about your partner may come from observations of his or her family life. A solid, warm and caring family might provide a solid plus for your choice.

Successful Choosing: Eight Factors

The following eight factors are important for you to consider when choosing a partner. How you handle them could make the difference in whether your intimate relationship is successful or not.

1. **Attractiveness**. Certainly attractiveness is an important factor. You should be drawn to being with your partner. But attraction, while important for passionate beginnings, needs to be more than a physical experience, because a person's physical appearance will change with age.

2. **Caring behavior**. This is expressed by interest in each other, by saying things to praise, console and comfort, being present when needed, and wanting the best for each other.

3. **Conflict management**. The ability to resolve issues without a belligerent attitude, to be more interested in finding ways that promote *win-win* settlements rather than *win-lose* ones, to be able to listen to each other's complaints and wishes, to compromise major differences to find solutions that do not leave each

other badly hurt—all of these are all necessary skills for a successful relationship.

4. **Sharing interests and activities**. If you love classical music, reading and intellectual discussions, it's easier if your partner does, too. If there are differences, then how well you accept them will make the difference. If one loves sports and the other loves dancing, then taking turns at participating in each other's interest or enjoying the difference and allowing time for each other to pursue them helps to keep relationships intact.

5. **Sharing values**. If your family is the most important thing to you, you want your intimate partner to feel that way, too. If you're concerned about money, you hope your partner will be conscious about costs and financial security. Value differences, because they represent intense commitments and can be a major source of difficulties in relationships.

6. **Flexibility**. Rigidity in insisting on "my way or nothing" can engender resentment, hurts, conflicts and hostility. A willingness to bend a little, to be experimental and try something new, helps a lot.

7. **Openness in expressing feelings.** You need to know how your partner feels about shared experiences, to feel that he or she can discuss issues honestly and openly, so they can be resolved rather than harbored with resentment.

8. **Trust**. Above all, you must be able to trust each other, to feel you can rely on what each other says and promises, to be able to believe in each other's honesty. Promises that are never followed

up by actions destroy trust. Another aspect of trust is feeling that you will always be protected by your partner and never feel that your partner would want to deliberately hurt you.

You may feel there are additional factors for success in choosing a relationship. If so, your choice should be added to this list and included for consideration. It's of primary importance to be assured of those qualities and factors you have decided upon in advance of any long-term commitment. When they are ignored at first and missing later, you may experience pain and regret. You may also find it difficult to terminate a relationship because children and other people are involved.

When You Haven't Made the Best Choice — Other Possibilities

The chances for a successful relationship are highest when a choice is made that takes the above eight factors (plus any other essentials that you have added) into consideration. However, many people make choices that do not result in a successful relationship. If this is your situation, and you are living in a relationship that was not the best choice, there is still hope! Of course, you will have to be thinking in terms of new possibilities and come up with creative solutions to make your relationship work.

The following are some possible paths to a successful relationship, even when you haven't made the best choice of a partner.

1. **Changing the structure.** Sometimes strong differences can be minimized if you don't insist that you both have to agree on everything. By dividing areas of responsibility and granting the

other partner the major decision-making power in those areas, conflict can be seriously reduced. The most difficult relationship is one where both partners insist they have to agree on everything. Some couples alternate choices: "This week, we'll do what I want, and next week we'll do what you want." Some allow for considerable differences in many areas but have defined the areas in which they have to agree.

2. **Adjusting to differences.** Partners in one couple we know have very different interests. He is introverted, enjoys reading and intellectual discussions, while she is bright and extroverted, and enjoys taking part in group activities, such as dancing. In fact, some of their differences attracted them to each other. However, he eventually resented having to go to parties where he couldn't dance, because he'd never learned how. She was bored by having to spend so much time at home. Both sensitive people, they were aware of each other's growing dissatisfaction with the marriage. After some discussion, he agreed to take dancing lessons and accompany her occasionally to parties, and she agreed to join him in learning French and inviting some friends to be part of a book club.

3. **Accepting some differences.** Another couple lived in the same building as the mother-in-law. She and her daughter enjoyed talking with each other and had always been close. When the husband would return home to an empty apartment, his wife was often with her mother. He began to be resentful and would sulk, seldom smiling when his wife was present. This only

encouraged her to spend more time where she felt she was welcomed – with her mother. Upset about the deteriorating relationship, he decided he would try to join the discussions and share his views. The couple agreed to also provide some "alone" time for the wife's visits with her mother, but to reduce the length of such visits. He admitted how he missed his wife and wanted more time with her, an approach that worked far better than sulking, and withholding communication and good will.

4. **Sacrificing a need and finding another way.** Passion created a marriage that was deeply intimate between a wealthy widow and a cash-poor carpenter. The husband was always aware of their financial differences and tried his best to provide what he could within the limits of his salary. He feared that his wife might take offense if she felt he was taking advantage of her wealth. A crisis occurred when she wanted to go on a cruise for a vacation, and he stubbornly refused. When he flatly stated he couldn't afford it, his wife solved the problem by replying, "I have the money, yes, but it's only worthwhile if it helps us share and enjoy what it can bring!" In other words, she made it clear that she was freely giving her money and didn't see it as her husband's taking advantage of her financial status.

In another instance, the wife earned much more than the husband. A divorce came about because the wife felt a husband should be able to take care of the wife on his own. She couldn't give up that fantasy wish for such a husband, nor accept a solution such as the one that the wealthy widow provided for her partner.

Self-Awareness Helps You to Choose

Cultivating the habit of examining your feelings and actions, so you come to know yourself can help you to make successful choices. For example, if you know that you are someone who needs to be in control in a relationship, it's important to recognize and consider that need in your choice of a partner. If you don't make choices out of such self-awareness, it may be a conflict to live with someone who also likes to be in control, unless you're willing to consider structuring events in such a way that both strong needs can be satisfied. If you tend towards being more indecisive and know this about yourself, you may want to choose a partner who takes charge.

What's important to you? What do you expect from your partner? What are your hopes and wishes? Does your potential partner agree and want to meet them? What does your partner want? It would be most helpful if both of you know yourselves and your partners well before beginning a long-term commitment.

Unconscious factors may also influence whom you see as a desirable partner and choose to enter into an intimate relationship with. You may "want a girl just like the one who married dear old Dad," as the old song goes. You may want someone who doesn't represent a trace of either of your parents, yet not realize why. You may find some puzzling things in your own behavior and attitudes and not know why they are happening. If you experience extreme relationship difficulties and they are repetitive, it would be advisable to consider therapy.

In a new book, *Your Mind May Not Be Your Best Friend*, Authors Vogel and Rosen describe how we are influenced by experiences and forces that aren't always known. They write of a man who experienced discomfort and tension whenever his partner became too accepting and supportive. As a child, the man had been constantly criticized by parents who expected perfection. Now, married to a non-critical partner, someone who was totally unlike his parents, he couldn't understand why he felt so uncomfortable, as if he somehow didn't deserve the caring support of a loving partner.

Imagining New Possibilities

In some instances, people who made choices that were not successful tried to resolve their issues and still found themselves unable to achieve satisfaction. Divorce may be an appropriate option, but hopefully couples can expand their imaginations and explore new possibilities first, considering the usually negative consequences of divorce.

As a practical exercise, see if you can identify at least three alternatives that might be helpful to the following couple scenarios. Do you see any chance for these couples to develop a better relationship? Write your answers here or in your journal.

Scenario #1. "Making Do" in a Boring Marriage. In this kind of arrangement, two people meet but there's no excitement, even though they may like each other. But they are essentially unhappy, both feeling they couldn't find anyone else. There's an offer and even though one or both are not feeling sure about the choice, they go out together and eventually decide to get married. That's what we call "making do," an arrangement that sometimes works but often results in partners feeling bored by the relationship.

What possibilities exist for such a couple? List three possibilities:

1._____
2. _____
3. _____

Scenario #2. The Age Difference. Consider an instance where there is a large age disparity. A woman marries a man who is 20-30 years older than she is. It looks good to her in the beginning, especially without examining what it might look like later in the marriage. In much rarer instances, the discrepancy might be reversed with the woman being older, but the same issues would arise, perhaps being exacerbated by the unusual character and fear of losing attractiveness with age.

What possibilities exist for such a couple? List three possibilities:

1._____
2. _____
3. _____

Scenario #3. Looking For The Perfect Mate. She thought she had found him—her perfect mate. He was looking for the same thing, but over time, neither of them measure up to the ideals of the other. Now they spend their time longing for the other Mr./Mrs. Right, instead of enjoying each other's company.

What possibilities exist for such a couple? List three possibilities:

1._____

2. _____

3. _____

Maintaining Emotional Health in Intimate Relationships

Up until now, we have focused on how to choose an intimate partner and what to do when that choice doesn't lead to marital satisfaction, causing problems to arise instead. Let's look now at some characteristics of an emotionally healthy marriage and what it takes to maintain that relationship, so you can build endurance and stability over the long-term.

Relationships need to be managed. By management, we mean acting in ways that lead to the achievement of goals you may have for the relationship. It does require some discipline and won't happen by simply wishing it to be so! Such a notion might seem strange when you talk about emotional bonds, but look at the behavior you already exhibited during your courtship: dressing in a way you felt would impress your partner, paying attention to needs, expressing statements that showed your admiration or affection, and acting in caring ways. In short, you deliberately chose behavior that would win a potential partner's regard and affection. In this way, you were attempting to "manage" the relationship, so you could capture the other person's heart.

A distinguished vice president of a telephone company, Art Leazenby, once said, "If you can't manage anything, you have to be able to control it. If you want to be able to control it, you have to measure what is happening and make corrections when needed." He meant you have to begin by being clear about your goals and periodically assess what happens on the road to achieving them. This applies to intimate relationships as well as to business ventures.

Sharing goals. Remember the expression concerning goals, *If you don't know where you're going, any road will do,* quoted earlier? Many couples hope and expect that their relationship will be ideal even though the goals of each partner are left unstated. We have seen how the choice of partner can be an unconscious and highly emotional one, not necessarily logical, realistic or practical. Such choices are often accompanied by ideals and standards that obscure the true nature of the other person. There is an assumption that we are joining together for sexual compatibility, comfortable ways of living, having children and mutual support. But are these truly shared?

However, there are many sides to a relationship. How you decide to deal with issues can make for satisfaction and happiness or create bitterness and tension. What goals do you have in your relationship? Ideally, this would be the result of joint discussion with an attempt to identify signs of success in reaching mutual goals.

Identifying goals. Making a list of such goals would be the first step—being realistic about the goals would also be a major requirement. First begin with simple lists and evaluate the practicality later. Defining goals in concrete terms makes them more achievable. It's one thing to want a nice home, but what is needed to meet that condition—when do we ever have enough? When can we feel comfortable enough to enjoy it?

Set goals mutually. It's important to set goals without one person dominating the choice, even if the other person is willing to go along with it. A goal should be a *mutually unreserved agreement,* so that resentments are not incurred simply because one person dominated. It is not often that every couple will agree on every item. Indeed, it may make sense in the process to include goals that are to be met by one person or the other, so there is not only couple fulfillment but personal fulfillment as well. Partners can also help one another establish personal goals that are meaningful.

A forthright example of such personal goals was written by Dr. Philippa Kennealy in a recent newsletter to members of an online network:

- I don't want to miss out on more of my child's life than I need to (allowing for some healthy separation!).
- I don't want to spin my wheels doing stuff that others could do more effectively and efficiently for me.
- I don't want to let one day slip by without acknowledging at least one good thing and one accomplishment during my waking hours.
- I don't want anyone else defining my accomplishments. Only I get to decide what they are and aren't.
- I don't want to lose valuable time and momentum berating myself for my flaws and failings unless it is truly essential.
- I don't want to choose based on fear.

Sample Marriage Goals of One Couple

- To resolve differences when they arise by first listening to each other and then striving hard to find something on which we both can agree.
- To share equitably in the various household and parental tasks that arise so that neither person feels unjustly burdened.
- To assure that we spend some time each year on a vacation.

- To have most money held jointly but for each of us to have a private sum for our own use.
- To support each other for adherence to diet and exercise goals.
- To make sure we save or invest money each month for our future.

Identify goal priorities. Unless you establish priorities, some goals may become lost or subjugated to other goals. It might have been important for a couple to have children, but their path became dominated by a constant striving for money and careers, and children never came about. What happened in that case? How does the lack of children diminish satisfaction with the relationship for one or both parties? How did they forget to pay attention to the goal of parenthood? Is it possible the goal was important to one of the members and not the other? Often we may make the assumption that what is important to us is of importance to our partner also. However, it's worth checking that out and listening to the answers.

Measuring goal progress. Goals not only need to be stated, but their achievement needs to be measured periodically. Goals may also change over time, necessitating reviews. It may have been important to have a summer home at one time, but medical and educational needs have come to require a greater priority.

Goals need to be both romantic and realistic. Without any romance, a relationship tends to wither—you are simply roommates. Without attention to reality, even great romances may run into trouble (lack of finances, dealing with repairs, assuring health, etc.). It is easy to forget some of the romantic goals that were so important at the outset of the relationship, such as trying to please each other, being attentive in one's appearance, being affectionate, expressing appreciation for what the other person does, celebrating special occasions, and preserving opportunities for some private moments and adventures. Reviews of both kinds of goals should also occur periodically.

As strange as it may seem, even romantic acts may need to be scheduled. For example, couples who make it a point to find at least one thing a day to praise in each other rate their relationships as much happier than those who rarely or never do so. We were surprised to hear a friend say he had been married for more than 40 years, and he and his wife had never said "I love you" to each other! Not having special dates for mutual enjoyment also diminishes the romantic spark. It may seem contradictory, but romance lasts longer when romantic behavior is planned and measured.

Reality requires scheduling. Acting as if you have an infinite supply of money means you're probably going to fall short sometime. Better to budget and keep yourself on a schedule that helps you control money. Realities like insurance, periodic visits to the doctor, keeping track of school progress, arranging for family reunions all flow more smoothly when they are part of a plan. You needn't be rigid about such planning, but the realities should be checked against some standards, as well.

Compromise when major differences exist. Agreements don't need to be made about everything, and when there isn't agreement, compromises can be made. Couples can decide to alter their individual preferences, so that there is satisfaction for both. An example would be: "You can go sailing Saturday, and I'll meet with some friends." Or, "This time we can go to the movie you want to see, and next time we'll go to one I would prefer. However, in choosing furniture, we'll buy only something we both agree on."

Measurement and feedback needs to be periodic. It is easy to let the years slip by and feel resentful for things that haven't taken place, to be reluctant to talk about things that bother you only to let them become a big block to satisfaction. As a couple, you need to practice opportunities for feedback, for sharing your views about how goals are being achieved, how you wish your partner would behave, for providing comments about the impact of behavior that may have been hurtful. There is no better way to do it than making such reviews habitual. Even better is being willing to express your feelings and wishes at the time a significant event occurs—to maintain an openness that fosters dialogue.

Progress reviews should identify positive outcomes as well as failures. A review is not simply a cataloguing of complaints, but a discussion that includes at positive as well as negative things, reflects a desire to *understand* rather than to blame, and is oriented towards increasing the quality of the relationship. A hen-pecked husband never realized that his habit of cutting his wife off when she was speaking built up anger that was expressed in her constant complaints, until after they had visited a marriage counselor.

Framework for a constructive review. This can be as simple and straightforward as describing:

1. Qualities I admire in you.
2. Things I have liked that you have done for me.
3. Things I wish you would understand about me.

4. Things I wish you would pay attention to.

5. Things I would be willing to do for you if you asked.

6. Thinking about our goals: What things do we need to pay more attention to? What priorities do we need to change?

Partners could also discuss what each could do to change how they handle romance and how they handle reality. Sometimes the request may be simple, such as, "I need a hug every now and then." And sometimes quite complicated: "We never seem to have any time to visit my parents."

Look at the following list of complaints and ask yourself whether any of them occur in your relationship. Place a check mark next to expressions you have spoken or heard from a partner.

____ "My husband never compliments me when I dress up for an occasion."

____ "My wife only concentrates on talking about the kids but doesn't show any interest in what is happening to me."

____ "He tends to discount everything I say, often interrupting me while I'm talking."

____ "He neglects his appearance and leaves his clothes around all over the place."

____ "He hasn't told me he loves me since the day we were married."

____ "She subjects me to a constant barrage of complaints."

____ "We never do anything except sit around the house or go to the movies."

____ "I wish he would take more interest in what's happening with the kids."

____ "Why is it only me that has to take the kids wherever they need to go?"

___ "Why can't he be nice to my parents and make them feel welcome when they visit?"

___ "She spends an awful lot of money on clothes that she wears only once."

___ "He spends lots of money on his hobbies but won't pay for repairs that are needed around the house."

___ "He seems to like sex but isn't really affectionate!"

___ "You have to be so careful about what you have to say to her."

___ "She always manages to say something critical about me when we have guests."

___ "He forgot it was our anniversary!"

___ "We always vacation where he wants to go—where the kids and I want to go doesn't seem important."

Discuss any persistent complaints. We're sure you can add to the above list. These items and others like them should be the topics for your review discussions. Many people are afraid of such talks. They may feel their weaknesses reflect a fundamental inability to love properly or to be worthy of love. They, like you, may wish their partner would simply provide complete acceptance for whatever they did.

Complaints are at first overlooked or tolerated, but when they persist, failure to be attentive and a reluctance to join activities and have fun may be the consequence. Accept the fact of your differences and that they *may* affect the other person negatively. This is quite normal, but if they really bother you, then make some attempt to solve the problem.

Resolve issues early. Remember that the earlier you resolve such issues, the less they will impact on your relationship. Some couples have found it useful to prepare an agenda and give it to the other person prior to the review.

It is important to accept each other's needs as valid and not to dismiss them, even though *it is not the way you may feel.* There has to be time for both of you to express how you feel and what you want. You may have to negotiate terms and compromises to find a satisfactory solution.

Really hearing what is said. The purpose of holding a review is understanding and change. The most constructive thing to do is *listen* before you reply. It takes some risk to be able to tell someone how you really feel. If the other person starts to deny what you're saying, offers a defense, or doesn't pay attention, then an important opportunity to be intimate is lost.

Your first response should be to find out what is really being said. This involves paying attention not just to the words but the meaning and feeling involved. It is essential to understand how things look from your partner's point of view. Then, you should reply in some way that reflects your understanding and deals with your partner's concerns. In short, it is an emphasis on *you* that's the most important part in listening. When you and your partner both listen more intently, it is easier to find solutions. Blaming and emotional displays occur most often because someone feels nobody is listening or even wants to listen.

Make sure you find out what your partner really wants. You may not always be able to provide satisfaction, but you may be able to negotiate some changes that ease the tensions. Sometimes that may mean a trade-off—you'll do something your spouse wants, and she'll do something for you. You can't always have what you want, and if you always win in such situations of differences, the other partner will begin to lose interest in you and the relationship.

Follow up your decisions in subsequent reviews. If you haven't done what you promised, then find out why not and see what needs to be done to make the change happen.

Guidelines For Problem-Solving

As a result of your sessions together to set goals and have periodic reviews on the progress of your relationship, you're going to want to solve problems that come up. Here are some important guidelines to follow when you undertake achieving changes and solutions.

Don't get locked into only one way of thinking. C.F. Kettering, an American inventor, engineer, businessman, and the holder of 140 patents, was fond of telling a story about someone who argued with him that it would take more than an hour to go from one particular city to another. "I'll show you," Kettering announced, and arrived at the destination in a mere 37 minutes. The other person then said, "But it's not fair, because you didn't take Route 23!" Kettering replied, "There's more than half the world on either side of Route 23!," meaning there were any number of routes you could take other than route 23 to get to the destination faster.

Sometimes you can get stuck thinking that there's only one solution—*God knows, I have always done it this way!* But more likely, there are many solutions, and it pays to always be careful to examine your assumptions. Try to think of some alternatives before making a decision based on what you think you know. *Explore the possibilities!*

Think about what can be changed and what can't. Don't expect miracles and major changes to happen in another person's life, such as when asking someone to change careers. Be content in getting your partner to express more caring. Realize each partner has some inadequacies that are unlikely to be changed, accept them and focus instead on the admirable qualities. Be careful not to label the other person as never being willing to change. Such an attitude often becomes self-fulfilling.

Think about the price(s) you pay. You may be able to get your spouse to give up a night of bowling, but you may also earn a lot of resentment. Is it worth it? If you've made the decision not to make such a request, don't revisit the issue! You may get your partner to go along with something you want, but if it's important, make sure it's an unreserved agreement, not simply a compliant one otherwise you'll pay the price of resentment and lack of commitment. Too many "Oh, I forgot" statements are signs that some objection was never voiced or heard the first time the issue came up.

Satisfying Five Important Emotional Needs

How emotionally healthy is your relationship? Emotional health can be measured by how important each individual's needs are fulfilled. Consider the following five basic emotional needs and how they are met in your relationship.

1. The Need To Feel Important. Each of us wants to feel as if we matter to others. As children, we experience that we matter in different ways, from the amount of time our parents spend with us, the extent to which our needs are heard and met, things that people say about us, and the displays of our images and achievements. If you have no opportunity to express your views, if no one listens to you, if things that mean a great deal to you are ignored, if no one greets you when you enter the room, if people keep you waiting for appointments, if people ignore you when you are present yet constantly talk to others, you will probably get the idea that you are not important.

When you don't feel important, it is hard to have a positive sense of self-respect and confidence, to feel capable of fully expressing your strengths. You may despair, become hurt, angry and depressed. Think of how many ways you show your partner how important he or she is to you, from the time you arise until the time you retire.

2 & 3. The Needs To Feel Respected and Accepted. Each partner needs to feel respected, knowing that his or her views are heard, recognized and accepted. When belittling and critical comments are made without reflecting a positive valuing of the other person, disrespect is experienced—a sense of rejection that can be quite profound.

When you ignore things that are important to your partner, it often breeds resentment. People want to feel that others see them as sensible and likely to have good reasons for their positions, even if they seem counter to your own. A positive way of expressing a difference to your partner might be, "I can understand that issue is very important to you, and that you feel you've experienced it often. However, I'd like to add something to the discussion and see how you feel about that." In this way, you show respect and still are able to make your point. More importantly, a statement that acknowledges the worth of the other person makes it more likely that your point will be heard in turn.

Inviting everyone in the family to participate in making decisions shows respect, especially if their points are restated and considered. Diverting conversations from areas being discussed is often interpreted as disrespect. Failing to give credit when the other person is right is similarly discouraging and harmful to the relationship.

4. The Need for Inclusion. It's essential that partners and family members feel included in many areas of decision-making. It is also important to be clear about who needs to be involved in such situations, even if one of the partners is largely responsible for that area. Consulting before acting and including the input of the other person(s) demonstrates both importance and respect. Even in areas of child care, sometimes including children in decisions (e.g. where to go on a vacation) heightens the feelings of being included. This also relates to sharing information that affects the other party.

5. The Need for Security. Everyone needs to feel safe. In an intimate relationship, feeling safe means you can count on your partner to be there for you. You can count on being protected against outside forces. You can feel safe and comforted when you come home. (In another part of the book, we shall discuss financial security.)

Consistency is one guarantee of security. When we know where our partner is, have ways of getting in touch when needed, and feel trustful of the tenure of the relationship, we can feel secure. When treatment is considerate and caring, it helps build security. When comfort can be given to anyone who needs it, accompanied by reassurance that everything is okay, security is nourished. One marriage partner reported that he never felt safe, because he couldn't predict whether his wife would be nice and caring or terribly frustrated and angry when he came home.

By fulfilling promises, you contribute to a sense of security, making others able to predict what will happen. While circumstances can occasionally disrupt this, living up to your word generates trust and assurance, as well as communicating to your spouse and family that they are important and respected by you. This is even more important in the case of divorced families when a parent is not available when expected. Don't make promises if you know you may not be likely to fulfill them!

When something happens that creates an emergency, knowing help is there or on its way creates security. Undue delays, especially without updated information, are likely to be viewed as unreliability and seriously undermine the feeling of being safe.

Anticipate threatening events and be prepared for them. Your partner and other family members will feel more secure if they know there are plans for taking care of unexpected events. Insurance provides a major form of security, even if it is never needed. A caution may be to avoid over-exaggerating negative consequences. This can create apprehension and despite its intent, insecurity. It is important to attend to a partner's or child's fears to minimize insecurity (e.g. failing to provide an alarm system for the house, not purchasing a safety helmet for bike-riding, etc.).

Don't take unnecessary risks. Taking risks without preparation may also be harmful. A sailor friend loves to sail at an extreme angle of heel, despite the fact that it terrifies those who are not experienced sailors. He even allows his son to sit on the bow rail at those times, despite the possible danger. A major risky investment in the stock market may jeopardize security in the event of downturns.

Keeping Your Relationship Alive

Following are some reminders that can help keep a relationship emotionally healthy and alive. If these are issues in your relationship, commit to making changes that reverse any ill effects you have been creating by forgetting their importance.

Integrity and being yourself. In every intimate relationship, partners have a desire to make each other feel happy and to receive enjoyment from what each does for the other. Indeed, we feel pleasing each other is an important part of being emotionally healthy in an intimate relationship. However, too do this and feel false, not to express reservations or make your needs known, doesn't build intimacy and can actually stimulate resentment.

It is easier to live with someone else when you feel you can be your own person—free to make your points and express how you feel. You need to trust that you won't have your views dismissed, even though differences exist. The differences can be productive, especially if there are equal feelings and the couple can look for a mutually satisfactory resolution.

If you can't feel that way, if you feel love will be lost if you are open and honest, then fear will prevail. This fear will lead to a loss of real intimacy and a loss of love. Blaming and critical behavior will then appear—a sure sign that people feel terribly threatened.

The emotionally healthy aim of an intimate relationship is not to quell differences, but to respect them and find ways they can be resolved.

See the comical part of life. Sometimes when events seem most tragic, it may help to view the event as a comedy—to see how funny it might look to others.

Unresolved differences. Some differences may still remain—strong couples find ways to assure that the solution is not always only one partner's way. It is sometimes helpful to take turns doing things the way the other person wants. In some instances, areas of responsibility are divided so that each partner can have an area where they are in charge.

As we mentioned earlier, if the premise in a relationship is to change the other person, then it is a poor one for maintaining a satisfactory relationship. Major changes are difficult at all points in our lives, and to insist that change be worked on constantly makes the relationship a struggle rather than a joy.

Knowing what differences exist, accepting them and yet trying to work with them is healthier. It also avoids the terrible frustration of failing to see the changes occur. That doesn't mean that couples shouldn't try to do things that don't deliberately offend or annoy the sensibilities of the other, but it does mean that each member should understand the strain that is involved.

It is also important to realize that habits are strong and lapses that occur are not acts of violation. Otherwise you develop the awful feeling of being let down by your partner—in extreme, this can become a kind of paranoia. A common fault in such change efforts is the constant nagging when failure occurs. Criticism becomes all too frequent. This is especially destructive when negative behavior overbalances any praise for efforts made to change. The balance is a healthier way to live and reminds us again of the importance of showing respect and caring for each other.

The "Law of Revenge." Psychologically, it is probably true that each act of unkindness (criticism, ignoring the other, forgetting what can hurt, etc.) is likely to be followed by a strong desire to get back at the offending person—to take revenge. While this is natural, an excess of this behavior can be ruinous, depleting the love and caring that made the relationship prosper. Certainly, there are some hurts that can almost founder a relationship in and of themselves—e.g. infidelity or betrayal. However, if the couple continues living together, they will have to have such an event forgiven rather than live with constant rancor.

The price you pay for unhappy relationships. For some couples, joy and interest has withered. They spend their time trying to make each other miserable, sometimes by being guilty, other times by accusations and finding fault with everything, even grim silence. What an unpleasant possibility! *Why would anyone choose to live like that?* It would be far better off to terminate the relationship and allow each other the possibility of enjoying life again. It is understandable that having children might change the equation, but often the underlying hurts and angers get transformed into negative feelings toward one or both parents.

The healthy relationship strives to create as much joy as possible for each partner, where you enjoy the happiness your partner receives from events, even though those events may not be joyous for you.

One woman, who suffered from constant parental battles, desperately wanted her mother to divorce the father and free the children from the constant acrimony that dominated the household. However, the mother acted as if she believed that by continuing her marriage, she could make the husband suffer. It is hard to see a life dedicated to getting back at the other person as a worthwhile one.

Leaving the unchangeable alone. It is very important to stop carping about things that cannot be changed and make some decisions about what else to do. There must have been some good points in your partner's favor, so concentrate on those and enjoy them. A constant nag isn't appreciated, even when justified. Focus instead on what can be changed and have more peace of mind. That will not help the perfectionist who must find paragons of ideal behavior, but it will help those of us who are more pragmatic and see the overall relationship equation as more balanced and capable of some joy.

Imagine what happens if your partner were incapacitated by illness—certainly you would have to make the best of it. If a career is lost—what other alternatives are there? What could you do about it? Usually there are more possibilities than you can imagine. One of our fathers lost his job during the Depression. His wife, who was an experienced bookkeeper, wouldn't consider the possibility of working, because it meant she would lose status in the eyes of her family and friends. This was a lost possibility! For years, her husband had to work two or three jobs to make ends meet.

You might want to think of some possible solutions for situations that feel almost overwhelming—Let your fantasies play! The value of finding a solution(s) is that by doing so, you can have even more satisfaction in your coping efforts. Moping, feeling sorry for yourself, wondering why the fates have chosen you—all these when carried to excess can be deleterious for emotional and physical health.

Sex Matters: Self-Education Concerning Realities

Generally, good sexual relationships are assumed to be a part of marriage—an implicit guarantee of satisfaction with a partner of your choice with whom you have been romantically involved. In the beginning, sex tends to be frequent and intense but fades afterwards for many partners.

Appetites vary. One partner is easily aroused and expects frequent contact, assuming the other partner feels the same way. In another couple, one or both partners may have less frequent needs. As in other matters, both people need to share their feelings about frequency, the kinds of things that arouse them most, and some of the things that turn them off. Prolonged knowledge and intimacy may not require as frequent sexual contact as occurred initially. Couples should be prepared for this natural change and not necessarily view it as an indication of failure or waning love. Sometimes one partner may not feel terribly aroused yet desire the other to have some satisfaction. This, too, is a kind of love.

Sexual problems caused by other marriage problems. When a partner has been active and involved, and then loses interest, it may be a sign of problems that have to be discussed and resolved. It could be something physical, but more often psychological issues arise in sexual matters. When people are disappointed, angry, feel hurt and overlooked, sex can be perceived as a burden and the joy lost. Some discussion after disturbing incidents can allow for exploration of feelings about such issues.

Sometimes an issue can become so intense—for example, the case of a woman who desperately wants to have a child and cannot. There may be a desperation associated with sexuality, resulting in a need to schedule activities to coincide with fertility. This may make a husband feel he is being used as a child producer rather than seen as a lover. If people have long standing disputes, the bedroom may sometimes be a place to overcome them, but more likely, arguing in bed creates distance and loss of interest.

Misleading cultural myths about sex. Our culture creates expectations of sexuality that may not be met. Here are a few myth-busting truths:

- World-shaking orgasms don't always occur with each encounter.
- Everyone else isn't necessarily having better sex than you.
- The man is supposed to be responsible for initiating sex, but some men who are less aggressive may be expecting the woman to be the initiator.
- There can be differences in sexual appetites, just as there is for food. Sometimes stimulation of the other person may be

appropriate, even though you aren't fully turned on.

- Men are automatically aroused, able to become erect and be forceful—true for some men but not all. One possibility is that the woman may have to be more forceful, with both parties accepting this rather than resenting it. Some male illnesses and hormonal differences may be responsible, for example high blood pressure, prostate medications, testosterone levels, etc. Not understanding this, a woman could be resentful, criticize her partner's inability to be aroused and imply that he is not a real man. Others can explore possibilities for enjoyment without penetration—e.g. oral and or manual stimulation.

- Women don't have to have an orgasm to be fully satisfied. Some women are not readily capable of having such an experience and yet still love their men. Sometimes this may occur because the man does not know how to provide the stimulation needed by the woman, something only a candid discussion can reveal.

Seeing sex as part of loving and caring. When sex flows naturally from involvement and caring, it is more likely to result in satisfaction than when partners merely go through the motions. Otherwise, couple sex is only masturbation, a condition that one writer described as, "spurts of loneliness." Sex then becomes less prominent and significant as the measure of couple success.

Respecting each other. Recognize the differences and the strengths of your partner. Focus more on them than the deficiencies. It is very hard to feel turned on by someone who is constantly criticizing the other or pretending that sex can solve all kinds of problems. If your partner doesn't want sex at the exact moment you do, grant him or her the right to abstain without your feeling rejected.

If this is always the case, however, something must be wrong. An amusing story may be appropriate: A man wanted sex and was experiencing difficulty with his partner. He yelled at her, "I want what I want when I want it!" She replied, "You'll get what I got when I give it!"

Appreciating what each means to the other. When each person feels the other can see his or her good points, communicate approval and liking, provide recognition for what is given, and take pride in the other's accomplishments, sex becomes more of a natural accompaniment to those good feelings.

Sharing fantasies to heighten romance and sex. Good sex can sometimes be helped by variety and play. A couple can build a fantasy game and then convert it into reality by acting it out, from a "date," a meaningful event, special roles, and an imagined sexual encounter. After all, these are common fantasies. You and your partner may both feel foolish at first, but practice will make it easier and allow both of you to participate wholeheartedly, even though you may begin awkwardly. You can also share fantasies about an imagined lover and then act out a rendezvous.

Planning vacations and being in more erotic situations. Sometimes a trip to a remote island, a tour of some exotic place, or a fancy bedroom can stimulate erotic behavior. Try to include such events in your life. They can make both of you feel special. Take some vacations with your partner alone, not always with others.

Marital rape. In some couples, the lack of desire is met with force (usually by the man) to get what one partner wants. Such behavior is demeaning and creates fear and tremendous hostility. It is as if one is continually being beaten to have sex. This is not an example of emotionally healthy behavior and the "victim" should find some way to stop the behavior, even if it takes legal means to do so. It is equally unhealthy when physical force, intense threats, and beatings are part of the relationship.

When Conflicts Arise: Fighting Fair and Other Struggles

The ideas of George Bach, author of *The Intimate Enemy or the Art of Fighting Constructively in Business and Marriage,* are helpful in addressing discord in intimate relationships. Dr. Bach felt that couples should be respectful of certain rules in order for fair fighting to take place, enumerated as follows:

1. **No foul blows.** If you know your partner gets hurt and can't take certain criticisms, such behavior is not allowed.

2. **No "museum piecing."** Everyone has memories of what the other partner has done or failed to do. If you insist on bringing up old faults, then you have to give equal time for the other person to mention what they remember. You will usually find each of you can present almost as many items as the other. Therefore, don't waste your time.

3. **No physical fighting.**

4. **Find out what is making the other person angry and why.**

*Listen***!**

5. **Try to find solutions that satisfy both of you.**

Other issues, such as power struggles, the drive to be right, differences in perceptions or memories, all call attention to the many pitfalls that we face if we choose to let them occur. In a recent Mayo Clinic Health Letter, researchers recommend slowing down, constructive discussion, not confusing anger with sadness, and Positive Sentiment Override (PSO) as helpful alternatives. In the Letter, PSO is described as "mentally stepping back from a situation where your partner may have annoyed or aggravated you, and realizing there's much more to love about your partner than to dislike." The Letter continues, "Although a particular situation may have made you angry, PSO can help you override or transcend irritation by recognizing the good in your partner."

It can be helpful to distinguish between your *intentions*, your *behavior* and your *impact*. Your intentions are your wishes, desires and motives. Your behavior is what you do, and the impact is the effect your behavior has on the other person. For example, you may question your partner about something, but your partner interprets your intention as anger—perhaps a very loud tone of voice was used, so the message became confused. Often when you understand your partner's intention, the negative impact is reduced, particularly if your partner can show you how a different way of behaving could have changed the interpretation. You then have an opportunity to alter the interpretation. This involves a willingness to let your partner know how you are being affected by his or her behavior and the willingness to listen to an explanation.

For some marriages, outsiders and professionals can be helpful. It can help to have an understanding and empathetic person listen to your feelings and wishes, and to help translate these into meaningful terms to each other.

Divorce, Too, Can Be Emotionally Healthy

What begins as joy and excitement doesn't always last. We are approaching a point in our country where almost half of marriages end in divorce. The pains of such separation are often traumatic, not only for the partners but for their families as well.

There are many reasons for divorce: infidelity, lack of financial support, violence and simply the experience of growing apart and no longer caring. The choice of ending a disturbed or dysfunctional relationship isn't easy, and many partners continue in such a state despite the misery experienced by one or both parties. Guilt about being the responsible party or being unable to satisfy the other person may make it difficult to take steps to separate. Fear of shame also plays a part— *What will others think of me?* In fact, such feelings may prevent full satisfaction in subsequent relationships, almost as if one had to suffer to atone for these feelings.

It is possible, however, to go through an "emotionally healthy" divorce. For this to happen, it is important that couples come to some understanding and agreements about finances, children, division of assets, insurance, etc., before lawyers get into the act. Since lawyers are committed to gaining the most for their clients, they often create more acrimony and a spirit of war than was ever intended. Each partner should monitor such aspects to avoid imagined hurts and hatreds, when no harm was intended. Ideally, the emotional healthy separation would be one where both parties wished each other well in the future.

When relationships have deteriorated into bitterness, when each partner constantly shows up the other party by citing the partner's faults to others, when there are outbursts of anger and recrimination, it is a strong signal to either seek professional help or make a decision to separate. Sometimes such behavior allows insights that lead to changed behavior and improve the relationship. Often both partners may realize how they contribute to their problems. This may not save the marriage, but can help in establishing better relationships with others and children.

Counseling and therapy, even if they don't save the marriage, may identify attitudes, often unconscious, that contribute to failure. Some of those attitudes are:

- Wanting someone to always be understanding and sympathetic like a parent
- Wanting someone to be constantly bestowing gifts
- Believing that each party should always be calm and never express any strong emotions
- Feeling that your own wishes should dominate decisions affecting the family
- Feeling that everything should be done together
- Resenting an independent pursuit of interests and activities
- Desiring constant reassurances that you are loved by the other person

Living with another person isn't always easy. There are differences that can cause irritation, ranging from how clothes are left, toothpaste used, vacations chosen, responsibility taken for children, etc. In a healthy relationship, you understand and accept this, make allowances for it and hope compromises will be made to allow each partner to feel reasonably satisfied. When fantasies about the partner prevail over reality, love is destroyed, interest in others heightens and the willingness to devote effort to working together diminishes. It is important for everyone to understand the underlying wishes and to realize how they may be helping or interfering with a relationship.

The consequences of bitter relationships profoundly upset children, making them anxious and often affecting school work and peer relationships. The children wish for a magical solution that would keep the parents together. Once a decision to divorce occurs, both partners should agree on how to present it to the children, reassuring them of continued love and contact, never engaging in criticism of the other party.

Fighting over custody can often be divisive and disruptive in children's lives. Nevertheless, there are often circumstances where the children have to be protected from a parent. Counseling for children may also be helpful if they appear upset by the separation and/or events that take place when they are in the custody of a parent. Ideally, the children should live with the parent capable of providing the most love, security, contact time and supervision. Because these are important decisions, in an emotionally healthy divorce parents will discuss them and try to agree on an approach that they can both support when talking with their children. Periodically, the parents should share information with each other about their observations of the children.

Establishing New Relationships

Establishing new relationships is often difficult for people after a divorce. If involved in such a circumstance, you may feel you are incapable of attracting a person who would want to live with you. You may feel hurt, disappointed and angry. Support groups can often be useful to reassure you, help you gain confidence in your own strengths, and understand who would be the most compatible partner in the future. In many cases, psychotherapy is helpful to identify attitudes that have worked for and against relationships.

Providing time for you and a new partner to become fully acquainted with each other is especially helpful. It may prevent you from repeating your previous mistakes. If you and your potential partner have already established families, it will require a longer acquaintanceship period to assure a meaningful relationship, since issues will arise not only from the interaction of you and your new partner, but from your children as well.

When a partner is lost through death caused by health problems or an accident, other factors may arise when establishing a new relationship: Will the new partner be seen as equal or better than the old one? Is the partner able to adjust or is a new relationship expected? Both of you need to respect old memories but also focus on the new relationship.

Despite desirable qualities of your partner, your children may naturally resent anyone who replaces their former parent. You can anticipate it will take time and love for them to make a meaningful transfer to your new partner. However, it is also important to allow your child to cherish their former parental attachment and to mourn the loss.

Beware of Guilt. Frequently, guilt can lead to overindulgence of children, especially if a child or children are only visiting. There may be reluctance to establish the kinds of limits that had been in place previously. This is not helpful for the children who gain security from consistency and shouldn't have to compare differences in treatment when being with either parent.

Living with stepparents can be problematic for children. No matter how warm and caring a stepparent may be, it will take time before the children are able to make strong positive relationships with them (unless they have experienced terrible relationships with their parents). The stepparent is likely to be seen as a competitor of the previous parent, and open resentment may be expressed or anger flare up over some frustrations later. Consistency in treatment helps, as well as support of the stepparent by the parent. *It is especially important that the parent helps create the legitimacy of the parenting power of the new partner* and does not simply side with the children because of guilt over the divorce.

In later years, problems also occur with grown children who feel that elderly parents have no business remarrying. They may hold this view because children feel romance is impossible in old age, or feel their inheritance is threatened by the new relationship. The new parents also have to build their relationships carefully. They also have to realize that for their relationship to succeed, they have to value it at least equal to their relationships with their children.

Summary

After reading this chapter, we hope you will feel it is of value to:

- Assess the state of your satisfaction with your partner, so you can live a life that provides optimum happiness for both and identify steps that will improve your communication.
- Develop attitudes that will enable you to accept and appreciate the differences between you and your partner, and to value each other's strengths without constant effort to change the other person.
- Consider the impact your behavior has on children, family and others.
- Periodically identify problems that need to be solved for mutual satisfaction and commitment.
- Give each other space to be yourselves and yet accommodate each other's key needs.
- Schedule time for romantic as well as everyday events.
- Not only discuss differences but commit yourself to carrying out the needed action steps to resolve them.
- Ensure that you deal with the satisfaction of the five important needs.

Chapter 4
Parenting

Every parent wants to be sure that their child's start in life is a physically and emotionally healthy one. But how can you be sure that what you are doing will ensure your child growing up to become an emotionally healthy adult?

The answer to that question is the subject of this chapter. In it, we will explore some of the wisdom accumulated in our own years of parenting—and what we know now that we didn't know then about emotionally healthy parenting attitudes and behaviors.

To begin, look back at your own childhood. Was it a time when you felt cared for and loved? Did you get support from your parents when you needed it? Or was your childhood full of bad memories: a household marred by angry adults, inconsistent and painful punishments, neglect due to parents being preoccupied with careers and daily problems? Did you often encounter fearful circumstances with no one around to reassure you? Hopefully, such bad memories—whether or not you had them in your own childhood—are not what you want your children to remember.

A Personal Assessment

If you are a parent now, the following assessment will be helpful in examining your behavior and attitudes toward your children. If you are not a parent, you are probably around children in some relationship, perhaps as an uncle, aunt, or God-parent. Use that relationship as the context for this chapter, applying what you learn to contribute to the children in your life.

When you finish reading the chapter, do another assessment using the same questions, imagining this time that you have made use of the material and changed your behavior to provide more emotional health as a parent.

Ask yourself the following questions and write your answers here or in your journal:

1. My greatest pride comes from seeing my child:

   _____

2. I would like to improve my ability to handle a specific problem with my child (children), such as:

   _____

   _____

3. As parents, we feel our greatest strengths are:

   _____

   _____

4. As parents, we need to improve:

   _____

   _____

5. On a scale of 1 to 10, I would rate my parenting as: ____
6. On a scale of 1 to 10, I would rate my partner's parenting as: ____

Possibility of a Positive Outcome

It helps to keep in mind that even the worst circumstances can have a happy ending. A story we are familiar with is that of a young woman who lost her mother early in life and whose father was absent. She was essentially reared by her grandparents, in particular her grandfather, who became her emotional rock. He provided advice when she needed it, helped her out of many difficulties, and in effect, became like a father to her.

On one Father's Day, he received a handwritten card from her with the following words written on it:

"Raised by a single parent with no father in sight."

To Grandpa:

A dad teaches you...unconditional love.

A dad picks you up...when you've fallen down.

A dad tries to protect you...from your own poor judgment.

A dad leads you to...the light at the end of the dark tunnel.

A dad makes you feel...beautiful, safe and secure.

A dad gives you...the strength to keep going when you've failed.

I've been good, I've been bad, and either way...

You've always been my Dad!

Happy Father's Day!

Thank you for being the *Amazing* You!

Love Always, Emily Rose

This heartfelt message from his granddaughter brought tears to the eyes of Irv, Emily's grandfather, when he received it. In spite of the many hardships life had handed his granddaughter, this message attested to the possibility of a positive outcome for both her and her grandfather.

What would you write about your parents? Would it sound like this card? What would you like your children to write about *you*? Take a moment and write in your journal a message of thanks to whomever raised you, in spite of the many difficulties you may have had in your childhood. Then write the message you'd like to receive from your child someday.

If Only...

A frequent topic among parents whose children are now adults is the regrets they have over mistakes made in the past. One of our friends recently said, "If I had only been more consistent and required my boy to work each summer, he could have had more respect for what it means to work for a living." Another friend reports, "I was so busy shuffling between my practice and driving kids to pre-school, I never really got to know them, and worse, they never really felt I loved them. We don't have a close family now – it's difficult to get everyone together on the holidays." A third friend with adult children remarked, "I was always so conscious of having my kids become the best they could be that I forgot how my critical remarks made them feel—they got the impression they could never satisfy me. As a result, they lack confidence and have difficulty asserting themselves with authorities, making it difficult for them to obtain the jobs they want." Still another remembers having always given in to her kids, because she didn't like conflicts and now realizes how spoiled and ungrateful they have become.

As a parent of grown children looking back, you too may have some regrets, but you also have some wisdom gained from your experience. You're likely to be much smarter now than you were then, as we certainly are. Let's look now at issues that arise in parenting and see how our wisdom can be used to offer possibilities for promoting children's emotional health.

Choosing Parenthood

One of the major issues in any marriage is the question of whether to have children at all. For many of us, it is a non-question, especially if we are adherents to certain religions. Children are generally viewed positively as a source of joy and satisfaction. Even prior to children's births, we think about their gender, discuss how we want to raise them, and develop plans for their future. As a prospective parent, you may have fantasies about your child's school progress, social connections, significant events, marriages, and even your future grandchildren.

Yet, some couples may not want children, feeling their lives don't allow for the time required to rear them. They may lack interest and skills in managing children and feel unprepared for such additions to their relationship. Rather than conform to the societal expectations, becoming parents who do a poor job and feel guilty about it, some couples choose the possibility of not having children at all.

For those who do decide to become parents, an immediate conundrum arises. Despite its importance, we are given little or no preparation for how to create emotionally healthy children, save for the experiences and memories of our own childhood. Presumably, society views this job as so easy that there is no formal training required to be a parent. We try to follow our roles according to what we believe will be best for the child, and fortunately, most of us do some things right. But we may be unaware of the effects that negative parenting attitudes and behaviors can have on the emotional growth of our children.

When you talk to parents and grandparents and ask them to reflect on their experiences, the stories are mixed. True, there is a lot of joy to report from interacting with cute, curious and charming children. There are also disappointments, conflicts, separations and tragedies. Many parents live with continuing pain over disruptions in their relationships with their children. It is common for parents to describe problems with their children in regards to discipline, flagrant disregard of rules, fights, disrespect, school problems, and many other heart-breaking incidents. It's no wonder that not everyone chooses this path!

Vital Questions

Ideally, if parents are to manage child-rearing, they would start by listing the outcomes they would like to see at different stages of development and the criteria that will be used to measure children's progress.

Here are some practical questions to explore when assessing your expectations as parents. In choosing parenthood, it is helpful for you and your partner to sit down together and discuss the following questions with each other:

1. Why do you want children?
2. How many children do you want? Any sex preference?
3. What do you expect from your children?
4. How realistic are the expectations? (It certainly doesn't make sense to expect a 4-year-old to behave like his 8-year-old sibling.)
5. What do you want most for your children?
6. What experiences would you like your children to avoid?
7. How much and what kind of time can you and your partner devote to your children?
8. What kind of resources can be used to help?

Emotionally Healthy Parenting

Children grow up emotionally healthy when their parents have emotionally healthy attitudes and behaviors in rearing them. You can develop emotional health as a parent when you are willing to examine your behavior and learn new approaches.

What are those emotionally healthy attitudes and behaviors? As we explore emotionally healthful attitudes parents can develop, we highly recommend reading *How to Raise Emotionally Healthy Children* by Gerald Newmark, Irv's brother. We referred to the five needs for emotional health from that book in our Chapter 3, when discussing interpersonal relationships.

Let's now review those needs as they pertain to our discussion of parenting. The five emotional needs of children that Gerald

Newmark cites are:

1. The need to feel respected
2. The need to feel important
3. The need to feel accepted
4. The need to feel included
5. The need to feel secure

How can you as a parent meet theses important psychological needs of your children? Below you will find several examples of how parents can satisfy each of these needs. There are five possible parental behaviors listed for each need, but obviously there are many more than are indicated.

You can rate yourself by indicating how often you do the listed behavior, using a scale of 1 to 5, 5 being *very often* and 1 being *rarely or not at all*. Total your points for each category. A score of 25-20 in any given category indicates you are exceptional in your ability to satisfy your child's needs. From 19 to 15, you are doing a fair job and need to pay closer attention to satisfying your child's needs. A score below 15 indicates you are not satisfying your child's basic needs and need to reassess you parenting behaviors if you want emotionally healthy children.

Answer again after practicing some of the behaviors that are suggested in order to measure your own development. Do you see any improvement in your child's behavior as a result of your practicing any of these possibilities? Discuss your progress and your child's progress with your partner or another family member.

The Need to Feel Respected is satisfied when parents:

1. Use praise for children's accomplishments and refrain from using ridicule or shame. ___

2. Respect children's private space and don't intrude, unless permission is granted or special conditions prevail. ___

3. Respect private discussions and don't reveal them, unless the child grants permission. ___

4. Avoid taking sides without providing the opportunity for all children involved to tell how they experienced the event. ___

5. Provide reasons for their actions and make sure children understand them. ___

   Total _____

The Need to Feel Important is satisfied when parents:

1. Are clear about wanting to have children. ___

2. Show concern about their children's welfare. ___

3. Provide acknowledgment for achievements that recognize the individual. ___

4. Spend time both in playing and learning with their children. ___

5. Provide physical and psychological help when needed. ___

   Total _____

The Need to Feel Accepted is satisfied when parents:

1. Listen empathically to children's opinions and feelings. ___

2. Show understanding for special interests and behavior. ___

3. Seek children's opinions and feelings and listen fully to them. ___

4. Recognize that certain behavior may be typical of growth stages. ___

5. Use welcoming and positive statements and don't use degrading

and rejecting comments. ___

Total _____

The Need to Feel Included is satisfied when parents:

1. Invite opinions and suggestions when activities affect everyone—e.g. preparing for a vacation—while setting some limitations, depending on the topic. ___
2. Share information with everyone who is affected. ___
3. Extend invitations for special events, so no one is left out unless special circumstances prevail. ___
4. Share unpleasant and critical events with children. ___
5. Hold special activity programs for all of the children. ___

   Total _____

The Need to Feel Secure is satisfied when parents:

1. Listen to fears and take steps to provide reassurance. ___
2. Provide relevant information about finances, protections, insurance and safeguards, as is age appropriate. ___
3. Provide regulations and rules for protection against risks. ___
4. Limit risk-taking behaviors. ___
5. Make expectations and consequences clear and enforce them consistently. ___

   Total _____

When you look at emotionally healthy parenting from the standpoint of satisfying children's needs, what do you notice? Certainly one sign of such health is that parents have chosen to become parents and regard their children as being important. You might also notice that emotionally healthy parents make sure there is enough money and room for children, as well as available time for interacting with them. In extremely large families, it may be difficult to provide a warm welcome, since each new child may be viewed as another financial burden and add to the sense of the family being too crowded. Nevertheless, providing sufficient resources for their basic well-being is an important aspect for the future emotional health of any child.

In addition, you might also notice that emotionally healthy parents have a relationship with each other that is characterized by some specific elements, such as the sharing of interest in raising their children; the willingness to share responsibilities in providing time, care and involvement; a common agreement about how children should be brought up; a willingness to collaborate on the transmission of values and discipline that may sometimes have to be administered. We would also expect parents to be partners in monitoring health, schooling and developmental aspects—all ways parents demonstrate their ability to meet not only their child's emotional needs, but their physical needs as well.

Finally, when we view parenting from the standard of emotional health, we see frequent expressions of affection and praise by parents for their children's behavior, as well as recognition of when children adhere to rules and achieve goals.

Important Warnings

While Gerald Newmark's five needs for emotional health as cited above can guide you reliably in how to act and interact with your children, some words must be said about how *not* to act. The following warnings are offered to help you avoid relating to your children in emotionally damaging ways.

Don't let your anger be the main lesson. It is particularly important that as emotionally healthy parents, you and your partner don't allow hasty, angry reactions to become the major lesson of an event. When the behavior of your child is displeasing, be sure to ask for an explanation and listen to him or her describe what happened. In doing so, provide evidence of caring as well as expressing your anger, explain your concerns, and tell your child how you believe he or she should have behaved differently.

Don't demonstrate disrespect for your partner. In addition, you should not ridicule or disparage your partner in this process, but demonstrate mutual respect and a collaborative approach when dealing with children. Failure to do so generates disrespect for the disparaged parent and often contributes to psychologically disintegration of the family, leading to actual physical disintegration.

Don't treat children as possessions. It is imperative that you treat children as individuals, not possessions or projections of yourselves. As emotionally healthy parents, you will also recognize circumstances when you cannot help your child and may need to arrange for the child to receive special care.

Don't ignore the effects of family changes. A final warning concerns how you deal with changes to the structure of the family, such as adoptions, deaths, divorces, and re-marriages. Be careful to encourage a sense of family by making an effort to help new members integrate into the original group. Failure to do so can leave damaging psychological effects, such as children feeling like they don't belong or are alienated from the family. The same applies to helping original family members adjust to the newcomers.

As parents, we are seldom paragons of virtue; more likely we are preoccupied in daily life with concerns other than our children, and therefore we make mistakes we later regret. For example, a problem at work may be dominating your life. Perhaps you received a devastating diagnosis of a health condition. Financial pressures may restrict your resources or make you especially sensitive to any extra costs that are incurred by a child. Fortunately, what a child remembers will depend upon the mix of total experiences, not only the mistakes. But if we are not careful, we risk falling into extreme parental behaviors that will be forever stamped in their memories.

Healthy Discipline: Rewards and Punishments

The emotionally healthy parent provides discipline that is both fair and makes sense to the child. The most common method of discipline is the use of rewards and punishments, doled out according to the child's behavior and whether that behavior conforms to what parents expect. This method can effectively teach correct behavior, but if misused, it can do significant emotional damage.

Emotionally healthy parents have goals for their children; there are a number of things they want them to learn. They also realize that children have different capacities for understanding what is required of them as they age. For an infant, the teaching experience could be simply pulling the child away from a threat, such as when he or she crawls too close to a space heater that is turned on. For an older child, parents can teach through reasoning about a perceived danger, explaining why it is important to keep a safe distance from heating elements that could possible burn the child.

Here are some quotes from adults we know about their experiences growing up and how their parents used—or misused—the technique of rewards and punishments in disciplining them:

My parents were always fair, although somewhat strict, and rewarded me for doing things well and punished me for things that I didn't handle properly.

My parents were models for what I should be. I learned a lot about what it meant to be a caring, responsible person.

My parents counterbalanced each other. My mother showed me how to be a loving and dedicated person, attentive to the needs and feelings of others, and my father showed me how to be practical and goal-oriented. Both made me aware of the need to behave ethically toward others.

Things were uncertain. I couldn't predict whether I'd get a hug or a slap in the face. It all depended on my mother's moods. My dad seemed to be out of it—he left all the disciplining to my mom. However, we were made to fear what he might do, since she always would warn us, "Just wait until your dad gets home and learns what you have done!"

My parents were very patient. They took time to show me how to do things, let me practice, and when I made mistakes, gently corrected me. They tried to explain why I needed to do something and, even when I received punishment, what it was for and why they had to administer it to me. The punishment was never severe but proportional to the behavior.

Rewards and punishments were erratic, sometimes too much for what was done, sometimes missing, and other times forgotten. It was hard to tell what was going to happen and my siblings and I often tested the limits by behaving outrageously to see what would happen.

My parents were mean. It seemed to me that they were looking for excuses to hit me. Life was fearful and anxious—I tried to stay out of their way as much as I could. There was never any hugging or close contact. I felt I was living with strangers. I couldn't wait until I was grown up to leave home. As an adult, I seldom visit them or invite them to visit me and my family.

Accomplishments meant a lot to my parents. They were immigrants and were hoping their child would have a very different life than they'd had. Although we had little, I felt they cared that I had enough. They emphasized the importance of being educated, and I was an excellent student, the pride of both my parents who would talk about me, almost embarrassingly, to others concerning my school records. They also read a lot, and at dinner we always had discussions of ideas and books. Their pride, warmth and joy when I did well, was all the motivation I ever needed. The only "punishment" occurred was their disappointment—if I didn't do as well as they expected.

My parents were perfectionists. Everything had to be done repetitively until it was right. Learning was a chore with little reward, save they would get off my back if things were going well. I did reasonably well at school, but they seldom offered me any praise for what I did. It was as if they constantly looked for ways to criticize—to always expect me to do better. Despite doing well in school, I felt inadequate, and each test was an experience of anxiety, lest I do poorly. The irony of it all occurred when I received my degree from MIT, and my mother smiled proudly, saying, "Well, we did it!"

We were poor and my parents were uneducated. Whereas some of my friends had parents who read books and newspapers, I experienced none of that in our home. We never went to a museum, library, or participated in any special learning activities—learning only occurred in school. At the same time, they were heavily religious and insisted we go to church after class to become moral people. They were concerned about us and wanted us to succeed. They were decent, hard-working people who loved their children and families, so we still see them regularly, but with regrets for what we never learned.

We're sure you can write your own story about how you experienced rewards and punishments in your family, and the lasting effects your parents' positive or negative behavior had on you. Depending on the parents' techniques, disciplining children can produce emotional health or it can do significant damage.

Let's look at how an emotionally healthy parent can use rewards and punishments in ways that create emotionally healthy children.

Healthy Uses of Rewards and Punishments

Rewards can be given in many different ways. In Chapter 3 on intimate relationships, we emphasized the importance of examining the ratio of positive to negative comments when talking with your partner. When talking with children, make sure that there is a balance in your communication to encourage him or her to feel good about achievements and to value your relationship positively. Compliments, especially when earned, have a highly positive effect and relate to the need for appreciation and recognition.

As a child gets older, rewards can also have other uses. They can provide something that means a great deal to the child, such as a first bicycle, a special trip, a visit to a cherished relative, or an opportunity to learn a new skill, for example going from swimming to water skiing or from studying to conducting research. The best rewards are opportunities for a child to grow in thinking and reasoning, and chances to apply something new that has been learned. As a matter of fact, the opportunity to choose a reward for an outstanding achievement can be highly valued.

The range of possibilities for giving children both rewards and punishments is limitless. Creativity can go a long way, especially when thinking of symbolic types of awards, like a special T-shirt, for example. Rewards for achievement can also be reflected in parental pride, especially when that pride comes from judging a child's achievement by child-appropriate rather than adult values. While tangible rewards will certainly be appreciated, your special recognition of something your child has done at school, for example, will probably mean more. These kinds of rewards broaden in meaning and have more lasting value. As children get older, they need less rewarding for their accomplishments, as they gain satisfaction from having met challenges and acquired skills that become inherent in what they know they can do.

Finally, if parents promise a reward that is within their means, they should deliver that reward when promised. Failure to do so can be disturbing to children and engender distrust, unless there are reasons explained. For example, if a promise couldn't be fulfilled because dad lost his job, a simple message can be communicated: "We know we promised you a new bike for your good behavior, and when we have more money we'll get it for you. In the meantime, let's think of something we can give you that won't cost so much money."

Guidelines for Using Rewards and Punishments

Emotionally healthy parents use rewards and punishments as possibilities to:

- Reinforce desired behavior.
- Build self-confidence.
- Promote judgment and perception of what situations mean.
- Increase learning skills for the future.

Increasingly, emotionally healthy parents strive to:

- Reinforce desired behaviors that are appropriate to the child's age.
- Be consistent in what is emphasized and rewarded.
- Provide a framework for understanding why the behavior is stressed.
- Enhance the child's sense of achievement and eagerness to increase interest in learning more.

Healthy parents *do not* consciously use rewards and punishments to:

- Express rage about children's behavior.
- Subjugate children to parent's control.
- Get revenge for the parents' feelings.

It is easy to be critical of many things that children do, but too much criticism without any praise creates resentment. You need to show your child that good behavior is also appreciated. Some families use stars and score sheets to acknowledge progress in following new behavior. Such devices may seem formulaic, but the practice of checking periodically to see whether new behavior is occurring and continuing makes sense. Changes should be noticed and praised, otherwise the child feels unimportant because there is no encouragement, only criticism. If a major change is sought, some sort of celebration may be a useful reward. If there is no follow-up on what is expected, try to find out why and adjust your responses accordingly.

Beware of Parental Excesses

When parental behavior becomes excessive—for example, exerting tight control over everything children do—then the results are likely to be harmful and cause serious strains in the parent-child relationship. A result of exerting tight control may be the child's over-dependency and resentment.

There is a close relationship between behaviors that are productive and helpful, and those that are overdone. Concern about a child's health is productive. Worrying about every little thing that happens or could cause a threat, is excessive. It is the moderation of the excesses—e.g. cutting back on too much control—that allows you to be assured you're on the right track.

An important key is how the child reacts to what you do. If his or her response is one of stubborn reluctance and resentment, you can be sure something is wrong—possibly a result of your having behaved excessively at some time in the past, if not now. Often asking the child how he interpreted the situation provides a clue as to what was overdone.

Whatever you do has an impact, and often you are not aware of what effect(s) your parenting has on your children. A poster that we saw some time ago captured how our behavior as parents has consequences for our children:

- The angry parent creates a frightened and angry child.
- A demanding parent creates a resentful child.
- A loving parent creates a loving child.
- A parent who ignores the child creates feelings of unworthiness.
- A parent who praises a child for accomplishment creates pride in achievement.
- A parent who won't listen creates a lonely and hurt child.
- A parent who insists that children do only what he/she wants creates dependent and resentful children
- A parent who has a sense of humor and likes to play creates playful and friendly children.

Remember, the negative behaviors and events described above can only happen when you develop patterns that are repetitive. A single burst of anger probably won't have a lasting effect (unless extremely violent), especially when balanced by warm acceptance.

Major Parental Excesses: Some Alternatives

It's important to understand how over-doing some parental behaviors creates stresses and strains for children and then think of alternative ways to accomplish your goal. Following are descriptions of some excessive behaviors to be on guard against, regarding *protectiveness*, *indulgence*, *control* and *intrusiveness*, with suggestions for other possible ways to handle typical situations.

Over-protectiveness. As a caring parent, you are likely to be concerned about dangers and making sure your children are safe. But if you constantly harp on the dangers that exist and restrict your child from outside contacts, he or she will become fearful and resentful, instead of cautious and loving. You have to provide protection but also provide freedom for the child to grow.

How do you know if you are over-protective? Signs of over-protectiveness can be measured by observing the differences in other parents' practices, as well as the comments of your own children. Do all the parents of your child's classmates let them ride bikes to school and only you don't?

You also have to be aware of your own fears, so that you don't breed the same fears in your child. For example, a mother was very afraid of dogs. When she saw a dog on the street, she would cross the street to avoid any kind of encounter. Her child grew up with an intense dog phobia and could never be around dogs. What else could this mother have done, despite her fear, to not engender the same fear of dogs in her child? Try to think of some possibilities. One is that she could have arranged for the child to have some pleasant experiences with a dog owner. Or she could have seen a therapist to work on curing her own phobia. Can you think of any other possibilities?

You can't always avoid harm, but you can provide resources for your child to cope when he or she encounters threats. Such behaviors as shouting, seeking help, or confronting the source can help a child to be safe. Teaching your child to avoid certain areas and persons may also help. Providing signs that indicate danger, such as a touch to the shoulder when the child steps off the curb to cross too soon, lets the child be alerted to precautionary actions.

Under-protectiveness. Just as over-protectiveness may be unhealthy, under-protectiveness can result in unpleasant and dangerous consequences for a child. Failing to set limits—allowing the child to do anything he wants—is not healthy. A child needs to know boundaries and warning signs.

Overindulgence. Certainly, you should try to provide what the child needs and some of what is wanted. Some parents however, interpret this as meaning they should never deprive their children of anything. The result is incessant demands, temper tantrums, inability to tolerate any delay in the satisfaction of needs, and selfish behavior. If you are seeing these behaviors in your child, you might consider that you are being overindulgent.

Healthy growth means having to accept some limits. Unlimited gratification does not prepare a child to cope with the social realities of living with other people. Some limits are useful—the child needs the adult to contain some behaviors. The child also has to learn some responsibility for taking care of him or herself. It is important to have to earn rewards rather than having needs and desires instantly met. This can become quite a problem in later life when children remain dependent and demanding of parents who no longer have the resources to provide for them. (See the discussion in Chapter 3 about providing for adult children.)

Over-indulgence can be an expression of parental guilt. This may be the case with divorced parents who feel responsible for the separation and try to atone by trying to give their child everything that he or she wants. This is especially the case for the parent who has limited access to the children and is trying to make up for the time apart by giving into every whim. This is not only damaging to the child, it is unfair to the parent who has the major responsibility for the child, causing increased tension in an already unpleasant situation.

Can you think of a possible resolution of this situation? It would be better for the guilt-burdened parent to examine the source of the guilt with professional help and therefore not have it be such a dominant factor in the parent-child relationship.

Under-indulgence. Some parents fail to pay attention to their children's needs, creating resentful and unsatisfied children who continually test the limits by trying to call attention to their needs. Such parental behavior often creates feelings of unimportance in the child. Deprivation may lead to depression and an inability to strive for goals. However, in a few children, this kind of neglect can lead to extraordinary achievements in adulthood, providing motivation to make up for the starkness of their childhood when their needs were ignored or situations made it impossible for them to attain gratification.

Over-control. Some parents want to direct everything that a child does. Such over-control places a heavy demand on the parent's time and further prevents the child from making independent decisions. As a result, over-controlled children tend to be passive and lack initiative, expecting parents to do everything for them. Occasionally, some may become quite rebellious, especially in adolescence.

A child needs limits but also has to have areas of freedom in order to grow into an emotionally healthy adult. Over-controlling parents may even attempt to decide what college a child should attend, the kind of career that the child should follow, the kind of spouse that should be selected, and later how their grandchildren should be raised. It is as if the child is valued only as an extension of the parents' own lives, leaving the child with a negative self-image and diminished sense of self-capacity.

If you recognize over-control in your own behavior—or that of your partner—what other possibilities exist for directing your children? Of course, examining your own psychological need for control, possibly evident in other areas of your life, would be one. Another is to offer your child more choices within a limited range of acceptable behaviors. For example, allowing the child to make a decision about when it is a good time to walk (wash, or feed) the dog, not *if* that choice is to be done. Offering clothes and food choices within parameters you clearly set can also be helpful in relaxing strict control and fostering more independence in your child.

Under-control. Some parents are reluctant to provide any control, often feeling that because they were over-controlled themselves as children, they would like to provide their children with more freedom. They fail to set limits or offer advice, and generally allow their children free rein. Children do need some limits and the opportunity to hear advice and suggestions from parents. Lack of parental control may result in children who are always testing the limits, insistent on having their own way—often behaving excessively to obtain direction and guidance. In some ways, these effects are similar to the case of under-indulgent parents.

Over-intrusiveness. In this instance the parent desires to know everything that is happening to the child, often feeling excluded and rejected when the child desires some privacy. This results in extreme behaviors, such as reading the child's mail, looking through drawers to inspect belongings, demanding reports of activities in detail, and often insisting on being present in all their child's activities. This is another instance where parental behavior can breed resentment. If this is a behavior you find yourself doing, think of some other possible ways you can become more involved in your child's life without causing over-intrusiveness. Also, have respectful conversations to get information so you don't feel excluded. Express sincere interest and you may find communication improves.

Under-intrusiveness. The opposite of over-intrusiveness is not exactly healthy, either. In this instance, children may feel the parent has little interest in them and wonder about how significant they are to the parents. Some curiosity in knowing about the child's activities is healthy, as long as it is not excessive.

Checking in with Your Child

Often we behave spontaneously and, if we're lucky, things turn out all right. It is rare however, save in extreme circumstances, that we think about the mark we have left on a child's mind from what we have said or done. Nevertheless, it pays to review our actions to find out how children viewed them and provide a basis for thinking about how to make changes in our behavior. Few parents want to deliberately create fear, loathing, disgust and disrespect in their children but may nevertheless do so when they behave in unhealthy ways toward them.

You don't want to become so self-conscious that you lose your spontaneity. Fortunately, most punishments are balanced by acts of love, but you should be alert when your children begin reacting in ways that signal trouble. Feedback from teachers, fellow parents and relatives can also be useful and needs to be evaluated periodically. It is necessary to be open to such feedback rather than react defensively to anything that is said negatively about your children. On the other hand, it is also necessary to be fair. The most important feedback is the reaction of the child to a particular event.

On one occasion, Allan was busy preparing a workshop when his then very young daughter inquired about what he was doing. He described to her how he was developing the technique of role playing in a training for business managers. To illustrate this, he asked his daughter to go out of the room and then come back in, entering the room exactly as "Daddy does." Following his instructions, his daughter left the room and then came back, opening the door and saying, "Hello. I'm home. Where's the paper?" Hardly the expression of a caring parent! Her giving him this feedback about his own parental behavior led to a change in how he expressed himself when returning home, reassuring his family that he was indeed interested in them, even though tired from a long day.

In another revealing incident, after Allan had criticized his daughter, she said, "Daddy, don't I do *anything* right?" Out of the mouths of babes! He had to think about what he was doing to his daughter's self-image with his insistence that she do things correctly, and also how he needed to supply more praise about behaviors he approved of.

These incidents reminded us of how important it is to ask children how they feel about their parents. You can do this periodically, either by asking, role playing, filling out check lists, or having a free conversation about what both would like to see more of and less of from the other.

Sometimes the results may be surprising. A young boy whose parents divorced experienced two different worlds, one with rather close supervision and another where the supervision was lax. When asked which situation he liked better, he chose the laxity of his father's home. When questioned further about which home he would like to live in if he could only live with one of his parents, he responded, "My mother's." While seemingly contradictory, his response makes perfect sense. Children may not like limitations, but they do realize the need for them and actually prefer situations that have the structure and safety that comes with sufficient adult supervision.

Dealing with Sibling Issues

Conflicts between siblings provide opportunities for parents to respond in healthy ways. Here are a few such situations with suggested possibilities for solutions.

Sick and Healthy Children. Sometimes children fail to realize why so much time is spent with a sick sibling and tend to feel rejected. This is especially the case with very young children who lack the skills to recognize what has happened. The sick child does require more attention, and the other children have to realize why—even to the extent of granting them some special attention and time. One youngster said, "I wish I had a bad heart like my sister so my parents would be with me more!" Sometimes providing some responsibilities for care allows children to feel more responsible and less jealous.

Favoritism. For many reasons, parents sometimes tend to like one child more than another and consequently relate more to that child. This can make other children feel rejected and less wanted, as if there is something wrong with them. It is important not to let such favoritism become excessive. The self-confidence of the rejected one can be severely damaged. Sometimes parents have attachments to one child that create a special bond between them which is highly rewarding. Nevertheless, it is important to strive for some kind of balance when there is more than one child in the family.

Sibling Rivalry. We all know of families where there are loving and warm relationships between siblings. However, when a newborn child enters the scene, it is natural for the older children to have some concerns and even resentment about how the new family member will intrude into their lives and territory.

Planning and forethought can help. How will the new child be introduced by the parent? Can the older child participate in thinking about how to welcome the new child? In one family, the older child was told his baby sister would be bringing a present when he arrived—and lo and behold, a much desired rocking horse arrived at the same time! Doing things together in dealing with the new baby can also involve the older child and develop responsibility.

While it is natural for the parents to be excited about the new baby, if total attention is devoted to the newborn, it may accentuate feelings of resentment. Parents should therefore make sure there is also recognition of the older child and his feelings. Hopefully, they prepared the child with information about the new baby and allowed for some expression of feelings, maybe even providing a special role the child could play in taking care of the newborn. However, normal feelings of rivalry can be exacerbated, depending on subsequent experiences with parents, and the amount of punishment and threat that has been involved in trying to change the child's behavior. It is important to recognize that the child is not being evil but only having natural feelings about possibly being displaced, even though certain behaviors are not permitted.

Raising Healthy Adolescents

Children grow up fast, and before you know it, you are dealing with issues of your adolescent or pre-adolescent children. This will call for new skill in practicing emotionally healthy behaviors that include the following:

Recognizing addictive behavior. In some families, drug addiction, drinking, bulimia and other self-destructive behavior occur, even suicidal attempts. This happens more frequently during the stressful period of adolescence, although some instances may pre-date that time. It is important to deal with the behavior early, rather than waiting until it becomes such an established pattern that it is exceptionally difficult to manage.

Parents should not make excuses for such behavior but confront it, preferably with professional help. Often such behavior is a cry for attention and help. Excessive secretiveness, unaccounted periods of time, and withdrawal are often signs that help is needed. What makes it difficult is the resentment that is often encountered when a parent tries to probe or make demands. Firmness helps but should be backed up with professional help. Highly negative punishment may provide some restraint but not a cure—firmness and tough love plus treatment is needed. The family should also guard against failing to pay attention to behavior or ignoring personal concerns.

Dealing with Sexuality. This is not an easy area for parents. Actually, the issues arise in childhood and are intensified in adolescence. Many of us have not fully settled our own feelings and attitudes about sex. The issue is further complicated by societal and religious views. Frequently, parents and schools fail to provide an adequate education in this area, so misinformation prevails and children are also subject to intense peer pressures, especially as they move into adolescence.

Interviews about how people acquired sexual information are revealing, as described in the following reports:

My parents were very secretive about sex. It was rare that we saw them naked. They felt we would learn what we had to in school or church. My mother was very concerned when as a young woman, I started dating. She insisted that there had to be a chaperon present and warned me about not permitting boys to take any advantage of me. I was very hazy about what sex involved, although friends provided some information. Unfortunately, one evening I allowed more intimacy than I had intended and became pregnant at the age of 17.

As a young boy, I knew nothing about sex until I went to camp. A counselor responded to some of our sexual jokes by gathering everyone together and given a fairly scientific lecture about sex. I was amazed and fascinated. I never knew that's how people made babies. My parents always seemed embarrassed when I asked them questions about sex and were furious to hear what I had learned at camp. At school, I heard about my friend's sexual adventures and experimented a little on my early dates. It wasn't until I was 20 that I had my first real sexual adventure, and I was a bit disappointed. It was only after I was married that I began to realize it could be so pleasurable and meaningful.

As a young girl, I grew up on a farm and had the chance to see cows and pigs born, even assisted during one of the births. My parents were very open about sex and provided a lot of information, so my curiosity was satisfied. When I described what I had learned to friends, some were shocked since they hadn't imagined what was involved. Some parents made some complaints, feeling that I shouldn't have given such information to their children. Although I knew about the mechanics that were involved, I didn't realize that girls looked forward to the experience, and it was okay to enjoy it – even to desire it.

My parents were very open about sex and answered any questions I raised in terms I understood. Despite this, my knowledge was somewhat sketchy, although my dad filled in the details when I became an adolescent. There was nothing that made me feel ashamed about my interests or behavior. Sex had been presented as natural, but my parents emphasized that it was a rewarding part of being in love with someone. I have tried to pass on that attitude to my own children.

Journal Exercise: Possibilities for Dealing with Sexuality

Think about your own experience. How did you learn about sex, from whom, and from what kinds of experiences? Was sex a forbidden topic, something to joke about in snide remarks, something to enjoy, or something restricted only to married couples? Would you want your children to learn about sex in the same way you did? If not, what would you do to give them a different experience? Write your answers to these questions in your journal.

Possibilities to Explore for Healthy Sexual Behavior

When dealing with your children on the topic of sexuality:

Give guidelines for sexual behavior, and be firm about limits—but with explanations that reflect loving concern.

Provide information when children's curiosity raises questions but at a level appropriate to the child's understanding. It would be ridiculous to provide a lengthy and detailed explanation about sex to a three-year-old, but appropriate for a teenager. If possible, try to provide sexual information at home, rather than letting children rely on peers as the major source, when all kinds of distortions can occur, and attitudes such as "macho-ism, taking advantage, forcing oneself or seducing others become the suggested norm for one's behavior. The advent of other children into the family may also be a meaningful occasion for informed discussions.

Communicate your own positive values. If you feel comfortable about your own sexual behavior, try to convey that attitude toward children, emphasizing the joy that accompanies a meaningful relationship. Have discussions about potential partners, share positive experiences that you and your spouse enjoy, and talk about important goals and a favorable family climate—all factors that can have positive consequences.

Offer your support if mistakes are made. Adolescents ought to be aware of the consequences of unprotected sex, and depending upon your religious training, prepared for any adventures. If your child gets into such a predicament as pregnancy, don't allow your alarm to panic the child but provide opportunities for discussion and counseling, sometimes with a professional. Be reassuring of love and help the child reach a decision that will have lasting positive value for him/her. Certainly blame, rancor and rejection are not emotionally healthy ways to deal with such an event.

Be inviting when your child acquires new friends. Get to know your child's new friends and have them get to know you. When adolescents feel that adults are interested in their relationships, they are less likely to feel the need to make decisions and act in ways that don't have parental approval.

Responding to Homosexuality. What would you do if you discovered your child was homosexual? Frequently, parents are shocked, disappointed and concerned, even reacting with anger. Some will reject and isolate the child, believing he or she has been exposed to outside forces that caused the homosexuality. One mother, whose son revealed at age 22 he was homosexual, simply cut off any future relationship with him, even though he was a brilliant student—Phi Beta Kappa and a Harvard graduate. For her, he was like a child who had died. In another instance, a father who learned about his 15-year-old son's confession beat the living daylights out of him and forbade him to continue.

Parents who are emotionally healthy choose other ways of responding. A mother, whose son was experiencing deep shame and guilt, provided the opportunity of psychological counseling to help him cope and decide how he might deal with his future. Other parents studied about the subject as much as they could, realized it wasn't simply a matter of choice but rather genetic, and tried to get advice about how they should handle the situation. Still others discussed their attitudes and feelings, told their son that they were indeed disappointed to learn about it, but appreciated their son's honesty. They then assured him they loved him and would do their best to provide support.

In one case, parents tried to discover the problems their son was experiencing and to find ways they could help, acting as coaches for him. When they first noticed an increased tendency toward isolation and effeminate mannerisms, they took him to a psychotherapist, believing it was mainly a psychological problem, but the treatment provided didn't seem to help. They tried strict supervision without luck. When at 18, he decided he was going to announce his status publicly, they held a party to celebrate the occasion as a demonstration of their support and love. At the party, one person came up to them and said, "I feel sorry for all that you've experienced," failing to recognize the meaning of what the parents had done.

But even if the parents' reactions are emotionally healthy, a revelation or discovery that a child is homosexual can be a source of constant heartache. If you have such a child, you may be concerned about how others will regard you and your child. You and your partner may feel frustrated when you realize your dreams for that child may not be realized. You will face constant problems of how to behave when meeting his or her friends and possible life partner. You will be concerned about how this information will impact siblings. Realistically, you may fear the possibility of your homosexual child being infected with AIDS. In addition, you would also be concerned about the pain and shame likely to be experienced by your child as a result of him or her interacting with people who cannot empathize with your child's sexual preference and lifestyle.

Most homosexual children realize they are different very early in life. They don't always share the interests of their friends and associates, and they experience some rejection and teasing from their peers. Often, they have been made to feel terribly inadequate by others' judgments. It is less apparent for girls than boys, but girls may experience lots of pressure when they exhibit a lack of interest in boys. They may also realize that this is something they cannot talk about with their parents and therefore feel terribly alone. There is often a fear by non-homosexuals of being preyed upon when associating with homosexuals, and especially the imagined possibility of contracting AIDS if they even touch a homosexual person.

As parents, you can, of course, feel life has treated you unfairly by inflicting such conditions upon your child. We have cited many things that constantly remind parents about their child's problem. That, of course, focuses on your feelings but not on the child's and your proper role as parents. The child needs to be understood as one likely to experience social shame, disgust, rejection and loneliness.

The situation is compounded by the fact that you may feel ashamed and apologetic for having such a child. You may feel that our friends are not likely to react with compassion and sympathy, but rather be judgmental and preventing their children from playing with your child, even making derisive comments. Others of the newer generations may be much more accepting as homosexuality becomes more socially acceptable.

Research indicates the primary influences in a child becoming homosexual are biological and genetic. However, in some instances, unfortunate life conditions, such as the absence of an opposite sex parent, may contribute to the behavior, and association with other homosexuals may contribute as well. Regardless, as parents you would still be faced with the need to help the child make difficult life choices and reassure him or her of your continuing love and support.

Again, if this has happened to you, and you have difficulty accepting a homosexual child, one helpful possibility would be to seek emotional support and understanding through a therapeutic intervention. You could also educate yourself about homosexuality and the alternatives available for parental behaviors that will be helpful to your child. Sometimes you might ask a non-judgmental relative or friend to provide help in mediating negative aspects of parental treatment.

The consequence of your rejection and disapproval can be that your child experiences everlasting hurt, anger, even suicide. He or she may have problems in relationship to authority figures and loss of motivation for pursuing educational studies. You might, as in the example previously cited, feel that you have lost a child. However, as a caring and loving parent, you would make every effort to be supportive and accepting.

Fortunately, we live in a time where homosexuality is becoming more accepted and integrated into all walks of life, including politics and business, than ever before. Indeed, this is changing even more as time goes on. Hopefully, this trend will lessen some of the difficulties we have described above.

Identify and Self-Concept

The issues of homosexuality lead us to a more general adolescent issue, that of identity and self-concept. Certainly how a young person thinks about him or herself is influenced by how others think about them, but it is also a matter of the amount of confidence they may have in themselves. Just because others may think you are lacking something doesn't mean you are. Indeed, in studies of sex, race, and body shapes, the pride and self-satisfaction a person may have has a primary beneficial consequence.

As a parent, you want to think about how you contribute to your child's sense of self—how your evaluations, acknowledgments and praise contribute positively to his or her self-development. Overly critical, deprecating, and negative judgmental remarks, when they are repetitive, can do much to destroy a positive sense of self, leading to feelings of inadequacy and even depression. In instances where a child suffers from social rejection due to some mental or physical flaw, you as a parent have to look at your own reactions to realize how you may be affecting the child, both unconsciously and consciously. Are you ashamed that your child is handicapped or disfigured? Any negativity on your part will be felt by your child, adding to his or her burden.

A sense of positive identity is also an issue that exists for members of various minority groups or special groups that may have been alienated from society. If that involves you as a parent, you have to help children feel positively about their particular group membership. At times, parents have to be a buffer between negative reactions of others and the child's feelings.

What are some other ways that you, as a parent, can help your children build self-confidence and a positive self-concept? Identifying and satisfying important emotional needs, as described earlier in this chapter, is a good place to start. Using rewards and punishment in fair, positive ways is another. There are lots of possibilities, so we invite you to use the material in this chapter to help define how you can contribute best to your child in ways that positively shape identity and build self-confidence for present and future emotional health.

Summary

After reading this chapter, we hope you will be able to:

- Realize the necessity for satisfying the five important needs of children and evaluate your success in meeting those needs in your child-rearing behavior.

- Recognize the specific strengths of your child and try to provide opportunities for him or her to use them as much as possible.
- Assess periodically how you can do more of what is healthy and less of what is harmful.
- Check periodically with children to find out how they are perceiving you and identify what they would like to see you do more or less of.
- Avoid the excesses of parental control and give children more opportunity to exercise their own judgment.
- Realize that children need containment for assurance and to feel protected from the consequences of their excesses—to set limits when needed.
- Realize that your children are not simply extensions of you but have their own unique qualities that need to be encouraged.
- Realize they are only children and need some adult help in dealing with issues. To provide time for counseling and guidance.
- Concentrate on giving them praise as much as criticism.
- Celebrate their developmental achievements.
- Allow them space to grow more independent as they develop into adolescence and beyond.

Chapter 5
Financial Security

Do you consider yourself financially secure? Your answer to that question depends not only on how much money you have in the bank or invested, but on your individual and highly personal interpretation of what it means to be financially secure.

The times you live in will also influence your assessment and can even dictate your happiness and the happiness of those around you. During the Great Depression of the 1930s, for example, Allan's father would come home every evening and sit at the living room window for hours, looking out at the streets and the hills. He would talk very little, except to respond to a question. No one realized that he was worried to death, feeling depressed and inadequate, because he might not be able to bring enough money home to feed the family, pay the rent, or God forbid, cope with a medical emergency that arose. He was terrified by the thought that he might not be able to make it financially.

Like Allan's father during the Great Depression, there are many people today who worry about losing their jobs, seeing their savings evaporate, facing foreclosure on their homes, and don't know where their next dollar is coming from. This kind of continuing distress and financial insecurity can lead to serious health problems and even suicide, as it did so dramatically in the Depression years.

We would hope that you never have to experience anything like what people faced in the 1930s, and in this chapter, we offer some suggestions to minimize the stress from today's financially challenging situations. Unlike during the Great Depression, when the entire world was plunged into financial chaos, there are many alternatives and possibilities to examine today for preventing anything so dire ever happening to you.

A Personal Assessment

Take a moment and write the answers to the following questions here or in your journal. Then, when you finish reading this chapter, do another assessment using the same questions, imagining this time that you have made use of the material and changed your behavior in regards to your financial status.

1. Rate your satisfaction with your financial status on a scale of 1 to 10: _____

2. What are you most proud of having accomplished to regards to financial security?

    _____

    _____

3. What three things do you feel you need to do to become more financially secure?

    _____

4. Rate your spouse's compatibility with your understanding of your family's financial security on a scale from 1 to 10: _____

Foundation of Financial Security

Financial security and emotional health go hand in hand. For you to be emotionally healthy with respect to your finances requires some fundamental practices, including that you:

- Be clear about your goals.
- Have knowledge of your finances and other resources.
- Create ways of tracking your expenses.
- Establish a set of priorities as guides to evaluating expenses.
- Are able to plan how to use money.
- Develop the discipline to stay within budgetary agreements to meet long-term goals.
- Have the flexibility to adapt requirements as situations change.

We have to recognize that for happiness, a certain amount of money is necessary but not always sufficient. A study conducted by the Princeton economist Angus Deaton and psychologist Daniel Kahneman revealed that the kind of happiness defined as *emotional well-being* or *day-to-day contentment* tended to be associated with income. As people earn more money, their happiness rises, but only up to a point. After they hit $75,000 a year, more money has no measurable effect on contentment. Increased wealth, in other words, does not make you happy.

While income can translate to happiness up to a point, feelings of insecurity and concerns about finances can severely influence your health in terms of loss of sleep, weight loss, feelings of depression, panic and anger. Think of the recent news story of a man who, affected by loss of his job, a divorce, and his inability to pay for much needed medicine, took a rifle and shot several people.

We must emphasize that in the year we are writing this, 2010, financial insecurity and anxiety are at an all-time high, reflected by the fact that more than 10 percent of the population is unemployed. It is challenging for those in favorable financial positions to put themselves in the shoes of the less fortunate, and there needs to be both governmental and personal attempts to provide that help when possible.

What Does It Mean to Be Financially Secure?

Being financially secure means different things to different people. You might say that both millionaires and bums have financial security; the millionaires, because they have loads of money, and the bums, because they don't have any money to worry about. Strangely enough, the founder of one of the world's wealthiest families, Samuel Bronfman, when asked how he felt after buying an $8 billion share in Dupont said, "I finally feel that the family is secure."

On the other hand, Irv knows a plumber who comes to the job in overalls, seems to enjoy his work, lives in a modest home, drives a modest car, travels as he wishes, occasionally eats in nice restaurants, and seems quite secure and happy. He has money in the bank, a small mortgage on his house, and an adequate emergency fund. What a difference in the attitudes of the plumber and Mr. Bronfman!

One man feels secure because he has earned more money than his father. Another feels secure because he's like the rabbi in the story who, when asked what he would do if his rabbinical job were lost, replied, "I can always teach." One woman feels secure because she has married an extremely wealthy man, while another, because she has a large sum earned from investments, savings, and a pension plan. A third woman feels financially secure because her profession provides a substantial income, and she feels she can continue working until retirement. At that time, she believes her investment income and social security will provide for her needs.

Personality Types and Response Patterns

How do you respond to financial upheaval and uncertainty when it happens to you or your family? Your response can correlate with your personality type, falling into four different recognizable patterns: *Passive Idealist, Independent Active, Deliberate Thoughtful, and Friendly Adaptive.*

Personality Type #1: *Passive Idealist,* characterized by trying to meet expectations of self and ideals, and often going along with others' needs and requests. The typical response pattern to financial crises for people with this personality type is to:

- Become depressed
- Blame self for failure
- Feel unable to cope
- Be anxiously seeking help and advice

- Be too willing to entrust financial care to others
- Become passive and dependent
- Be prone to ulcers and gastric diseases

Personality Type #2: *Independent Active,* characterized by a self-confident and optimistic view, willingness to take risks, and directive interactions. The typical response pattern for people with this personality type is to:

- Attempt to attack the source of difficulties to overcome problems
- Gamble and take risks
- Seek any possibility for gaining money without considering implications
- If everything fails, become seriously depressed
- Be prone to high blood pressure, heart attacks and headaches

Personality Type #3: *Deliberate Thoughtful,* characterized by caution, orderliness, attentiveness to details and analytical deliberation. The typical response pattern for people with this personality type is to:

- Pull back on any investments
- Watch money very tightly, be unwilling to spend – become stingy
- Take some losses to preserve capital
- Restrict activities and investments
- Be prone to constipation and diarrhea

Personality Type #4: *Friendly Adaptive,* characterized by an outgoing and positive outlook, flexibility and willingness to experiment, with a sense of humor. The typical response pattern for people with this personality type is to:

- Look to friends for advice and help
- Follow patterns adopted by successful people and friends
- Try to find some positive things to view – to use some humor to ease stress
- Maintain spending to keep up appearances and reputation
- Experience depression and also be accident prone

Do any of these descriptions strike home? What is the typical pattern of response for you when your financial security is threatened?

Sharing Financial Information

Lack of information can create financial insecurity, while information shared by husband and wife can provide a basis for future planning and decision-making. Unfortunately, in some families, one of the partners often enjoys having the role of financial planning and may even be reluctant to share it with the other.

In one family, the opposite situation existed. The husband was the sole financial supporter of the family, and when he attempted to share information about the family's financial status, his wife showed little interest. As a result, when he became ill his wife was panicked over how she would be able to get along without him if anything happened. This was her response despite the fact that the family had almost $3,000,000 in municipal bonds and stocks, as well as social security payments, all of it amounting to an annual income of $130,000 without the principal ever being touched.

Adding to the difficulty, the wife didn't know anything about how to manage the family's money, since she'd never become informed about financial matters. Hopefully, the husband had an adviser, but if not, she'd have to find one or suffer the consequences of making mistakes on her own.

As mentioned earlier, women may have their own way of assessing how financially secure they are. To be secure, one woman feels she must never be in debt, while another feels there should always be a continuous and constant stream of high income. One woman believes that she should never have to do without something she wants, while still another simply wants a roof over her head, money to pay medical needs, and some insurance.

For each person, men and women alike, what constitutes financial security is individually arrived at, and often has to do with factors of personality type, lifestyle, and even family background.

Family Background and Financial Security

Your family background can shape your sense of financial security, providing both attitudes you inherit as well as actual resources. Families that lived through the Great Depression may forever feel at least a twinge of financial insecurity, the impact of that event having been so severe and widespread. If you grew up while living in financially desperate times, and your family had to make the most out of every penny, then you would develop a very different attitude than someone who grew up in more fortunate circumstances. Because of your impoverished background, no amount of money as an adult may be capable of generating security.

Financial reverses, combined with all the obligations you have accrued, can lead to a terrible feeling of being overwhelmed and alone. The history of your family's financial experience may contribute: if resources were subjected to extreme fluctuations, you may feel less secure than someone whose family experienced a fairly steady and predictable income. Memories, whether conscious or unconscious, of how your family handled money may also play a part. The important point is that you bring your background into your financial thinking and ability to feel secure, for better or for worse.

Wise Planning Means Setting Financial Goals

Trusting to luck in building financial security is often disastrous. Therefore, it is essential to think of setting goals for your financial management. The goals should provide a sound basis for future planning, for dealing with emergencies, for using money to take care of needs, for providing for your loved ones, and for bringing peace of mind.

You may look at financial planning as an anathema. You feel that if you were to plan so soundly, spontaneity would be lost, because you'd be so tied up in thinking about money that you couldn't enjoy anything else. Yet when you're in financial difficulty, you look with envy at the person who doesn't have a large mortgage, is able to afford vacations, and can make a decision to spend money without agonizing over it.

When Allan was a university professor, his initial salary was low and had to be supplemented by outside work. He was reluctant to do any financial planning and resented having to contribute to the university's retirement plan, because it meant he and his family would have to live on less money. Surprisingly, when ready for retirement, he discovered he had accumulated $65,000 from that small investment. He would never have planned to do that on his own, despite the fact that putting aside a planned amount every month could lead to income during his retirement.

Would you be willing to take a small amount from your weekly pay check to set aside a savings or investment plan for your retirement? This may not be appealing to you, and so you currently don't do it. Yet, as Allan learned, it can be advantageous early in a career to learn to give up what appears to be a present benefit for the possibility of future gain and protection.

Do you have a retirement plan, one that will provide enough money for you to maintain your standard of living until you die? Do you know what kind of financial target and what kind of actions are needed to guarantee that financial security?

If money itself is your goal, you will never have enough, as illustrated by the Bronfman story. There will always be a higher and higher standard by which you will judge your financial security. Yet, if you don't pay attention to your finances, each new emergency will engender terror. This can be observed now in many families hit hard by the 2009 recession who had their pension money destroyed by stock market losses.

Of course, you can hope that you'll be lucky and hit the jackpot, inherit a fortune, or stumble on to some means of earning a lot of money. But hoping for those solutions brings a lot less emotional health in matters of financial security than does setting goals and acting to realize what you have determined you will need.

Plans that Create Emotional Health

If you want to ensure that your financial plans are guided by what creates emotional health, peace and security, consider taking the following measures:

1. Cover the basics. One measure is planning to have enough money to cover basic expenses, food, medical care, education, emergencies, retirement and funerals, as well as vacations and fun. How much money do you need now? How much will you need in five years? in 10? in 20?

Here are two journal exercises to help you think along the lines of covering your needs in the future. Write your responses in your journal and then discuss your answers with family members.

Future Scenario: Imagine you and your family are sitting in your living room five years from today. Describe the room and the house as you envision it. What would you say concerning your enjoyment of life over the past five years, and also your regrets over not having done certain things? Once you have written your answers, share your imagined scenarios with family members and discuss what you (all of you) need to do now to make the positive aspects of your vision become a reality. Then, do the same exercise projecting yourself 10 and 20 years into the future, based on having brought about the changes you want to see. What does that look like?

Paring Down: This exercise is especially valuable in current times when many are required to downsize. Imagine which of your material possessions you could do without—ones that might be lost and would have only minor effects on your quality of life. What changes could you make in your lifestyle, and still feel reasonably content and able to enjoy living? Think of all the things that are stored in your garage or attic—do you really need them? Could you be content not to have a new car every two years, to drive a Prius instead of a Lexus, to live in a condominium instead of a house, to wear last year's clothes, to have your children attend a public university instead of a private one, to have only one watch instead of four, etc.? What price, both emotionally and financially, do you pay for all those extras? How does your awareness of that price influence your future purchases and investments?

2. Financial knowledge. How knowledgeable are you about earning money? A sound career choice makes a difference. Familiarity with investments provides another basis. How experienced are you in managing money and making sound decisions about expenses? Does your family use a budget? Do you review expenses and revise financial plans as needed? Are you willing to spend the time and energy to be financially wise? Or in lieu of your own efforts, consult a financial expert?

3. Level of aspiration. It's important to set goals that have some reality of being achieved. To set a goal of saving millions is beyond most people's ability to achieve, but to reach a nest egg of $100,000 is probably within your grasp. An important thing to remember about goals is that *they can always be changed*. In fact, it's wise to make periodic revisions as circumstances change.

4. Goals that make sense to you. It is easier if the goals you set are ones that make sense for you, not others. Be cautious if you are easily influenced not by what you want, but by what others want. Measuring yourself against others' goals can provide some satisfaction in achieving a state of parity with others, but such efforts may impose a lot of stress and strain in the process. Keep your eye on the big picture: comfort, quality of relationships, mental and physical health—these should be your primary goals.

A discussion we had with a retired couple provided an interesting insight. "You know, we have lived in many homes, but our lives didn't change with each upgrade," they told us. "Now that we're retired, we find we're comfortable living in a two bedroom apartment instead of our five bedroom house."

Think about how catastrophes, such as the hurricane Katrina, earthquakes, loss of income, etc., can force you to consider what you can do without and still survive. How can you make sure you always have those bottom line necessities? What can you do in the event you don't have them? These questions are not only subjects for thought in the early stages of one's life but also for later stages as well, including retirement, illness and death.

5. Money for equal satisfaction. To keep stress at a minimum, couples should aim to arrive at their goals by *mutual consensus*, each party contributing to regular financial discussions. When needs are different, more than one set of goals can be constructed—something for one, something for the other, and something for both. One of our friends made a large profit on some commercial real estate he owned.

When he came home, he told his wife he planned to give her all of the profit earned for her own personal use, and he didn't want to know how she would spend it. Quite an act of love! Enough money should be available to assure equal satisfaction of needs.

Some financial goal-setting should include your children, as well as your spousal partner. It becomes easier to control expenditures in a family when all members have an awareness of why it's necessary to save money. When only one person is in control of every decision about expenditures, it can be detrimental to the marriage and child relationships.

There are both societal and personal differences in role expectations, and it depends on how each partner defines and accepts the role. In many marriages, the husband handles all the finances and the wife is dependent. Yet in a society where half the marriages fail, severe illnesses and death may require a change in roles, so it pays to assure that financial knowledge is shared. If not, then money is often treated as power, not as a means to live a secure and happy life.

6. Keeping track of financial information. Another measurement concerns records. Do you have a list of all investments, bank deposits, net worth of properties, financial advisers, etc.? To keep survivors secure, especially in a time of crisis, they will need such information.

7. Get help in managing your finances. You may believe that you should be responsible for what happens and therefore fail to be informed about options, legal and accounting issues, and other ways for accomplishing your goals. Having a trusted adviser to consult and review plans with can help. Make sure to verify their experience. You may also discover ways of handling events that you never imagined. However, don't let the "expert" do all your thinking, and make sure your partner is involved, as well.

Dealing with Financial Loss

If you want to have emotional health in your financial life, you must learn to view money as simply money—something to be gained and something to be lost. In cases of loss, we have found the following to be a good maxim: *Pay losses only once.* In other words, don't engage in repetitive thinking and obsession about an event that led to a loss, or you risk paying in emotional health—stress, worry, depression—many times over. If money was misspent, count it as one of life's common events, learn from it, and don't stew over it. We're sure those who trusted Bernie Madoff and other investment counselors without doing their due diligence learned not to trust someone with their money again, or to know what to look for that would assure such trust.

Remember, too, that how you react to financial losses will impact those around you, including family members. One father, with fresh memories of life during impoverished times, learned his son had spent $10 on a toy model and berated the boy for his "thoughtlessness." The son never forgot the incident, symbolic of his father's outbursts over unexpected expenses, and, driven by the desire to make more money, tried to always have more money than he needed. This occurred despite the fact that the family was no longer financially disadvantaged.

A lot of insecurity about money comes from the fear of loss, rather than the loss itself. Who hasn't had one or more of the following thoughts run through their mind with accompanying anxiety? *My God, what will we do if Daddy and or Mommy lose their jobs? What will happen to us if there's an earthquake? What if someone in the family suffers a major illness—how will we pay for it?*

Insurance plans participated in at work are obviously intended to minimize such threats and provide security. Alternatively, if you decide to self-insure, you will have to plan to save money for such contingencies. Some self-insurance plans could be devastatingly costly. Imagine the impact on your financial security if a family member had to undergo major cancer treatment and you didn't have any health insurance at all.

You may be surprised how easily you can let go of your desire to buy things when you've suffered a loss and be fine with what you have. Most of us want considerably more than we will ever get or need. In one child's experience of the Depression, the family had very little money. Because he rarely had money to purchase anything, the boy learned to love window shopping, entertaining himself for hours just by looking at goods in a store. Even in later years, window shopping provided more satisfaction than buying.

It's smart to suspect a spontaneous urge to make "impulse" purchases, lest you fall victim to persuasive advertising or sales of items you don't need. But every now and then, allow for your more spontaneous spirit when making decisions about what to buy. Having some "mad" money available for those times can make shopping excursions fun.

Planning for Your Gifts

Too often the matter of what you leave after you die can be left to chance, because most of us don't want to think about the end of our lives. But how you decide to reward people or endow organizations and charities is important, and will leave a lasting impression of what your life was about.

Make sure you have developed a statement of principles that justify the distribution of your gifts. The more people understand this even before your demise, the more secure they will feel. Some people, in a fit of anger, say many things they later regret. *If you don't do what I say, I'll cut you off without a penny,* is a threat you never want to say. Such a statement can create resentment and distrust, even when the person speaking never intends to follow through with it.

Consider your resources. Perhaps it would make sense to provide a gift before you die, so that someone in need can benefit now. This might be an outright advance or a loan to be deducted from their final inheritance. It would certainly be appreciated as an act of generosity and goodwill.

Sometimes even the best of intentions and care don't have positive outcomes, and you must consider some special instances. How do you leave money to someone who doesn't have the ability to manage it? A lump sum might disappear in a very short time. Choosing an executor or distributing money over timely periods can be more helpful. How do you provide for a child, spouse, or relative who is severely handicapped, suffers from psychological illness, or is otherwise impaired? Surely, you will want to consult with some specialists to assure that your heirs have the best possible help and care. Although, if you're a "do-it-yourself" kind of person, you may not feel this way.

There are also gifts that help others to help themselves, such as providing for the completion of an education or special work training. These are gifts that will last beyond the immediate endowment, impacting your heirs' lives in significant ways.

Making Final Arrangements

When a death occurs, surviving family members have difficulty making decisions about expenditures for the funeral arrangements and other costs. It is a time of heightened emotions and not the best time to make wise decisions.

In the event of your own demise, you can help your family by making pre-arrangements to provide financially for these necessities. It is difficult for young people to think about this, so by even saving a little each month for that purpose, it can be helpful for remaining family members. As a final gift to your family, remove a burden on them by taking care of things yourself.

Your Legacy

We have discussed your financial estate, but often there is more than money and property to be considered. You leave a legacy that depends on many things you have done in your lifetime. A major part of your legacy is the results of your parenting, in terms of how you have impacted your children's lives. What they will most cherish is the wisdom, experiences and opportunities that you provided: whether you have left them with a sense of kindness, generosity and love for others, as well as curiosity, and eagerness to learn and achieve according to the skills possessed. This is not just a terminal decision but something you will create over your lifetime.

Summary

After reading this chapter, we hope you will:

- Always set the level of expectations higher than your immediate needs.
- Make sure priorities are met—measure progress.
- Not get so trapped by money that you forget how to live.
- Have some money set aside for contingencies.
- Have money for fun, as well.
- Have an adviser in case of loss of a significant partner.
- Remember some losses are bound to occur. Don't sit and worry about them—act to make a difference.
- Remember that small steps can lead to big outcomes. Small sums, invested early and regularly can change your life later. For the sake of your later years, try to invest at least 5 percent of your income each year in savings.
- Remember that if money is your goal in life, you will never have enough, and less can be more.

Chapter 6
Work

Do you go to work because you have to, or because you enjoy your job?

For many people, a job is just a job, something they need to do in order to sustain life. At your work, you may work with unfriendly colleagues, toil heavily at hard tasks with little relief, spend many hours away from your family, and earn barely enough to do more than stay alive. Even when the pay is reasonable, the lack of satisfaction you may experience can extract a severe penalty in emotional and physical health.

Is this all we can expect from work, or are there other possibilities that lead to greater fulfillment and satisfaction?

Emotional Health at Work

For emotional health, your job should be a source of satisfaction and even enjoyment. Ideally, you have goals for advancing your trade or career, get along well with colleagues and bosses, discuss feelings and issues openly with others, and work on issues with an eye toward win-win solutions.

Imagine how different your life would be if this were the case!

Like in marriage, at work you expect there will be difficult times, disappointments and also improvements. You can cultivate an ability to tolerate such changes, understand what is happening, and not be completely passive about it. Sometimes, because of life events and choices you have made, you have to work at a job even though you don't enjoy it. At the least, you can appreciate the fact that such a job provides you with the means to enjoy other things in your life.

Exploring alternatives for work satisfaction when you are unhappy in your job and also knowing when it is time to retire and how to do it, are all indications of emotional health at work. In this chapter, we explore the many possibilities for work that are both rewarding and enjoyable, including dealing with important issues that can help you develop an emotionally healthy work life.

A Personal Assessment

Take a moment and write here or in your journal the answers to the following questions. Then, when you finish reading this chapter, do another assessment using the same questions, imagining this time that you have made use of the material and changed your behavior in regards to your work experience and satisfaction.

1. On a scale from 1-10, rate your overall satisfaction with your work, business or career. _____

2. What would it take for you to rate your work or business higher than a 7?

3. What are the areas of greatest dissatisfaction in your job or business?

_____

4. If you had it to do all over again, which career or job would you choose?

_____

5. On a scale from 1-10, how free do you feel to take a job that would provide more satisfaction? _____

6. On a scale from 1-10, how much does your job or business make use of your strengths and talents? _____

7. If you have your own business, how satisfied are you with its success on a scale from 1-10? _____

8. What changes would you make in your business to provide more satisfaction and success?

_____

_____

As you read this chapter, reflect back on your answers to the above questions and determine to make changes where you find they are needed. Then revisit this assessment and note how your answers may change.

Selecting a Career – Expanding Possibilities

Most people start out by making a choice of career or job and then get the training required. In an ideal scenario, you would have

enjoyed, he became highly upset and replied, "You don't understand. I need to keep working or I won't be able to retire!" Two years later, we received a photograph in the form of a Christmas card, showing the fishing business he had developed in a lovely seaside location. Like him, if you feel stuck, it may pay to explore other possibilities and not be cowed by doubts and fears, feeling your life is over before it's begun.

A Risky But Wise Change

Early in his career as a dentist, Irv found he didn't care for dentistry very much. He chose the profession because World War II was going on and dentists were needed in the military, and in his mind, dentistry was a better alternative than being a foot soldier. However, in his first year of practice, he found he'd picked the wrong career. Later, marriage and two children made it very difficult to change careers, and he continued on, acquiring new skills in managing his practice. He didn't give up in wanting to change and eventually designed a group dental practice that permitted him to use those skills that served him best and provided greater satisfaction on a daily basis. As a result, he not only created a successful dental practice, but he made a major contribution in health care delivery systems.

When those endeavors still didn't fully give him the career satisfaction he sought, Irv worked with his brother, a consultant, to see what other changes he could make in his practice. Together, they did a risk/payoff analysis to see whether Irv could work half-time and still support a family in the lifestyle they'd become accustomed to on his full-time earnings. As a result, some 35 years ago, Irv decided to not work both sides of the lunch hour—only half days. This arrangement provided him with the opportunity to add two additional careers to his life, that of lecturing to groups and writing on subjects in his field. Looking back, the decision to go part-time in his practice led to the satisfaction he sought, even though it was risky at the time.

If you are considering leaving your job because of a high level of dissatisfaction, it may pay to first consider how you could improve the quality of your life within your job. If that is not possible, another question to consider is: Can you afford to take the risk of leaving one job and seeking another? If, as suggested in Chapter 5 on financial security, you have accumulated sufficient savings and investments, you might have a cushion that would allow you to afford making such a change.

Romance and Reality in Work

Your choice of a career or job is vital. However, such a choice is easy to think about in idealistic terms. You may be disappointed when you face the realities. For this reason, you should be aware of work issues likely to occur at the job or career of your choice.

Even the best job has moments of repetition, tedium and frustration. An airline pilot may sit for hours, merely watching instruments instead of flying the plane. A doctor can be deluged with so many patients that he may not have the time to practice the best medicine. A teacher has to spend many hours preparing for classes. You are wise to know about and expect the realities that exist. If you simply fantasize about only the romantic highlights, you'll be doomed to frustrating disappointment and likely end up quitting your job often.

Regardless, you may have already chosen your career based on unrealistic expectations, a "romantic" concept of what you felt the job would be that engaged your fantasies. Indeed, you have to believe that a prospective job will be more of what you hoped for, in order to want to leave an old job. But too often, job-seekers don't do enough homework to make a realistic choice, failing to check with existing employees or find out about the organization, its procedures and organizational structure, the amount of supervision and other relevant factors. It's smart to have hopes but also to be realistic.

The Challenges of Change

Since both of us authors are still working at our careers well into our 80s, people constantly ask us, *When will you retire?* Our answer is pretty much the same: *If our health prevails, then we'll never retire. We enjoy what we are doing!* Even if we did retire, we would still be active, pursuing some aspects of our careers, writing and still learning new skills and exploring new ideas.

Yet we realize there are many people who do not experience such satisfaction and must work arduous hours without much psychological or financial reward. It's easy to say, *Try something different!* But if you are loaded with financial obligations, especially in the current financial times, what are the possibilities that exist for you to make a change? It may be hard to see, but our advice is to keep looking for possibilities and don't give up. There may be opportunities out there that are more rewarding, but you have to be open to see them.

Don't limit your search to what is familiar. It may help to look for some way-out possibilities, imagining a future that is very different, possibly involving a new form of technology that is still being developed. An example is an attorney we know who hated the drudgery of his practice and became so fed up, he went back to school to become specialist in literary analysis. Now his days are filled with reading the books he loves instead of poring over tedious volumes on law.

Gender and Career Selection

Many professional women who have children are often torn between home and work, yet their career choice is so rewarding that they need to work in order to be psychologically fulfilled. It is not an easy choice to make. Increasingly, women are well-trained and heavily invested in their careers. They face not only the problems men have at work but additional ones, often dealing with issues concerning their gender. Fortunately, there is legal support to combat discrimination, but the experience of it is not comfortable. Sometimes women find it's better to grin and bear it.

However, the following experience proves that a confident confrontation can often be more helpful than defeat or resignation. A manager was told she had to do something that went against her sense of the particular situation, and so she stated she couldn't obey the demand.

"Don't you realize that I'm the boss and can fire you if you refuse to do what I ask?" her boss threatened.

The manager replied, "I don't think you understand how a professional person functions. I can only give you my whole-hearted support if I believe in what you want me to do."

Her boss then countered with the following statement: "All right, don't do it! But don't tell me that you won't do it!" Sometimes confrontation of this kind can pay off.

Knowing Your Strengths

Choosing a career for financial rewards but not having the personal interest and skills to do the job well is likely to lead to disappointment and failure. One young man we know was a gifted writer, but his parents talked him into studying to be an engineer. After working for 10 years as an engineer, while continuing to write travel articles, he was lucky enough to be noticed by a publisher and has since quit engineering to make his career as a writer.

A young woman we know is working as a research chemist in a pharmaceutical company. She loves her job even though she is underpaid for the work she performs and the skills she has. In these times, she feels lucky to have a job and has never been confident, fearing to ask her boss for a raise, even though she is financially troubled and constantly taking out loans. With such an attitude, she will always be behind the eight ball. Knowing her own strengths, she ought to be confident enough of to ask for an adjustment and at least explore other job possibilities. What works against her and all of us is the feeling of comfort in a less than desirable situation, keeping us holding on to old friends and other familiar elements. It always feels risky to seek change.

A warning to parents: It's never helpful to pressure children into becoming what you want them to be or to follow in your footsteps regarding a chosen career. This is especially true if you can see that their talents, strengths and inclinations are elsewhere. This doesn't mean you shouldn't provide information about possible opportunities and question their choices. However, they are going to have to work for many years, and it might as well be work they enjoy.

Guidelines for Success at Work

If you work for a company or a corporation, there are several guidelines you want to follow in order to be successful in your job.

Become the solution, not the problem. To be successful at work in a corporation, you can choose to be a *problem solver* or a *complainer*. Problem-solvers win out every time. If something needs to be done, either do it or suggest the possibility and be willing to volunteer to help out. No one likes someone who constantly gripes, even though that person may be in the company of gripers.

Our own experience proves this out. Allan was appointed as head of a management development group, simply because he proposed a solution to a problem that had been of concern to top management. Irv formed a group of dentists committed to practicing in a cooperative way, rather than continuing as a single practitioner and simply wishing he were part of such a group.

Meet expectations of your boss. It's not enough to just complete an assignment. You are also likely to be judged by the way in which you did the work. Different bosses favor different styles of accomplishing tasks. You may have a boss who is highly organized and meticulous, and adheres rigidly to the rules. Even though you get things done, if you don't exhibit those characteristics, that boss will tend to downgrade your performance and be reluctant to promote or recommend you for raises.

Alternatively, you may function in a meticulous and organized way, but you work for a boss who values speed in responding to tasks, the use of quick judgment, and the ability to handle several tasks at the same time. If so, you would be in disfavor. A CEO who was a client of Allan's hired the brightest people he could find but was highly critical if they alienated colleagues and workers or failed to interact sensitively with customers. He valued getting things done well and smoothly more than just getting things done.

Your boss may value close and constant communication, even if he or she doesn't need to know all aspects of your job. Another boss may not be interested in hearing much from employees, unless it is an exception or something outstandingly bad or good. Again, you can always choose to meet your boss' expectations or not, but be sure you know the consequences if you don't.

In your initial contact before you are hired, it can help to interview your prospective boss about his expectations and standards, so you can find it easier to have your work deemed satisfactory. You may be so concerned about getting hired, you don't explore a valuable area that may be of paramount importance for your job satisfaction. So keep your antennae tuned to your boss' wave length, and try to meet his or her needs and styles without sacrificing your integrity. Be willing to modify your behavior accordingly, and you will find your relationship with your boss to be more rewarding.

Be flexible. It's also important to be willing to shift gears and try something else if you fail to find meaningful work. Management responds well to people who react to changes by becoming involved and helping to make the changes work well. As an asset when dealing with economic disasters, it can pay to have more than one set of skills in your repertoire.

Strangely, some people don't do this or don't realize that they have marketable skills. A retired colonel who had commanded a research base came to an aircraft company asking for *any* kind of job. Fortunately, a perceptive interviewer considered him for a management position where he could direct the work of a group of electronic technicians. Sometimes our less than positive self-concept can prevent us from taking advantage of opportunities.

Start a new job on the right foot. When you are entering a new work situation, it is helpful to show interest in getting to know colleagues and learning about their work and practices. Let others show you their expertise, rather than putting your own on display and attempting to enter as a star. One road to success is identifying the organizational and corporate objectives and doing your best to advance them, rather than advancing your own personal interests. Those who are competent and willing to participate in major efforts, and who work well with others are more likely to be valued.

Acknowledge contributions of others. It is surprising to discover how many people hunger for recognition and appreciation, even your boss. If you recognize that someone has performed well, tell them about it in detail by saying, for example, *That solution really opened up the possibilities for other developments*, rather than simply, *That was nice*, although even the latter is better than not saying anything. Bosses, too, need to have their behavior complimented when they have done something that has led to success. If you are able to recognize worth in others, they will probably reciprocate.

Avoid being the constant critic. No one loves such a person—indeed it often provokes anger and a desire to retaliate. People will also want to communicate more with you when you give generous with sincerely offered praise than if you seldom provide praise or encouragement. This is especially valuable if you are in management or run your own business.

Praising another's accomplishments is much rarer than you think. A study of management behavior revealed that they are 17 times more likely to criticize work than to praise it. Make sure you're at least equal in your distribution of comments.

Do your own job evaluation. Most jobs require a performance evaluation, whether it's a yearly review by a supervisor or a professional evaluation done by a colleague. But before that happens, do your own performance evaluation. Ask yourself: *What did I achieve during this period? How often was I able to use my strengths? How often did I volunteer to help others? How often did I express my ideas, feelings and opinions? What were some of the difficulties I faced?* For example, was there work that didn't get done to the satisfaction of your boss, colleagues or customers? Why did that happen? What can you do differently to improve your effectiveness? Some people have even found it valuable to share their own personal evaluations with their boss, invite comments, and commit to making needed changes.

Get on the road to promotion. A UCLA study of managers

showed that at the lowest levels, the primary quality sought was expertise. Middle managers, however, had to be skilled communicators as well as competent, and high level managers had to be able to relate smoothly with other colleagues. This information provides an important clue for what to do to get a promotion in your company. Don't just concentrate on technical skills if you want advancement—polish up your communication (both oral and written) and your social skills. Look for ways to gain more experience, to learn more, along with opportunities to apply such knowledge. Indicate to others that you are interested in trying something new. Volunteer for new opportunities at your job.

Cope with job stress. It's not good for your emotional health to stay in a job where you feel constantly under the gun. Being repeatedly criticized and/or shunned by your fellow workers can get you simmering in an internal rage. It is helpful, when in such a state, to take time out to gain some perspective. Having a good friend, an empathetic family member, or a trusted adviser to talk to can be therapeutic. However, be sure to choose someone who listens first before offering advice.

Another good idea is to examine problems early—don't wait until they have accumulated before you erupt like a volcano. Such assessments and discussions are often useful for finding productive ways of dealing with a situation. Even having the opportunity to share this is helpful and will relieve some stress; otherwise, not only you but your family will suffer. Work dissatisfaction and stress is also a prime condition for developing serious health issues. As in our discussion of financial security, you may have to look at the price you're paying (or your family is paying) for continuing on the job.

Enlist help to make a change. It is certainly valuable if your significant other can help support you changing jobs and make some of the sacrifices that will be required. In one family, the father was a small businessman who hated the daily routines, didn't care for constantly having to sell, and had become a pain to be around. He seemed to have lost his sense of fun, as well as his interest in his family, and was pessimistic about his life. Recognizing this, his wife, who had been a former computer programmer, volunteered to return to work. His mother-in-law consented to take care of the children while the wife was working, and as a result, the man was able to close his business. He had always wanted to be a teacher, so he found a part-time job for income while he returned to his university and eventually completed his degree. He is currently a high school teacher, his wife continues to work part-time, and family life is so much more enjoyable.

It is possible!

Starting Your Own Business

Frequently, satisfying opportunities are to be found in establishing and running your own business. In starting a business, there are several things to keep in mind:

Have a good knowledge of the business. It is essential to be aware of the relevant technology, the general business conditions, the competition, the potential profits and losses, and the investment that will be required. Too often, failure to invest sufficiently handicaps the business owner (poor equipment, insufficient staff, inability to pay for marketing and sales assistance, etc.). Since it's common to start with limited capital, you can become obsessed with expenses and fail to invest enough to have the resources necessary for building a successful business.

Create a business strategy. You need to know how to establish business goals, assess market conditions, identify competitive strengths, create a business vision, and measure progress.

Do sound business planning. It is essential to be able to identify what is required, create the steps to make the business prosper, organize your efforts, and make sure all the details are managed.

Know your strengths and the need to augment them. Except for a one-person business, it is essential to know what you can and cannot do, and when to use help. You may have all the necessary technical skills but not know how to market your product or service. Or, you can sell but don't know how to manage people. Don't ignore your limitations and what will be required to overcome them. You may be tempted to save money by hiring the cheapest help, but that often fails to be a wise move. Get the best help you can afford and make sure the people you hire are well-trained.

Be willing to risk. A major question you have to answer as a business owner is, *Am I afraid to fail?* If your answer is *yes*, then it isn't wise to start. However, in answering this question, evaluate what failure means. You may underestimate the risks, so take a look at the worst case scenario you can imagine. If you can't afford such a risk, it might be better not to start. Also, don't look only at the initial investment and don't be assured by early successes. They may encourage you to take even greater risks that put you in jeopardy. How would you feel about the risk associated with a tremendous expansion, where you might need to borrow a considerable amount of money and potential losses might be large? Would you be able to tolerate such a risk?

Working With Partners or Associates

In addition to the above, success in business often depends on how well you can work with partners or associates. Here are some guidelines for smooth working relationships and other considerations.

Identify compatibility. It's important to be able to identify if you are going to be compatible when taking on a partner or associates in your business.

Here are some important questions to ask:

- Do you and your prospective partner have common goals?
- Do you have complementary skills? What are they?
- Is the person cooperative or competitive?
- Do they have flexibility in accepting new or different roles?
- Do they have the ability to share responsibilities? (A particular point to consider is the need to control.)
- What will be the outside influences on this person, such as family members or friends? (Sometimes a spouse can be an unofficial partner.)

There are times when individual partners may be incompatible but have strengths that are beneficial to the business. Incompatibility can be dealt with by creating a structure to minimize it. For example, it would be destructive to insist that partners have to agree on everything. Where there are strongly controlling personalities involved, it would be better to divide the areas of business into separate sections, with each person being responsible for his/her own area. For example, in a consulting partnership with two powerful associates, the marketing and sales divisions were the responsibility of one partner and the business administration the other.

It is very difficult to operate a business with many equal partners. Often, this involves protracted discussions, especially when there is disagreement and may lead to unpleasant feelings. Often power issues may be involved. In such an instance, it would be better to identify a chief executive or managing committee to make the everyday decisions. There should be agreement about when decisions need to be referred to the total partnership.

Be able to sacrifice the present for the future. Sometimes partnerships fail because there is unwillingness to invest current earnings to promote the business through advertising, decorating offices, establishing credit policies or adding staff, because partners do not want to lose any current income. Consequently, the business growth is limited.

Make growth a source of satisfaction for everyone. If the work load becomes excessive, conflict creates ill-will and there are no opportunities for vacations or respites, then a partnership will begin to fail. You and your partners should strive to create a firm where you enjoy working, and everyone enjoys their relationships.

Be clear about terms involved when partners want to leave or accidents arise. Although it sounds unpleasant, such terms should be spelled out clearly and in detail, preferably during the startup period, so the partnership is not destroyed because of misunderstandings and bitterness. Important things to be considered are the worth of a partner's share, residual earnings that will accrue, legal rights of families, and future compatibility of newcomers. If you can't decide on those terms, you often can't agree on what it will take to succeed.

Retirement: Consider the Possibilities

If you have labored hard and experienced low pay on a job of little interest with disagreeable bosses, retirement can be a blessing. For most professionally-oriented people, however, ending one's career is something of a disappointment. Yet even for them, retirement may offer new realms for discovery and enjoyment, when hobbies, interests and past-times often offer new possibilities.

The following guidelines will help you to consider the many possibilities available for you at retirement.

Prepare for your retirement. It's wise to prepare for your retirement, both financially and emotionally, regardless of how you feel about working. You may want to do this with your marital partner, as well as your associates. What can you do, both independently and together to make retirement an enjoyable time of life? Few marital partners are prepared for a continual, 24 hour interaction with their newly retired spouses, so some preparation can smooth the transition.

Review your life. Do you want it to remain the same or change? This may mean moving to a more temperate climate or one that meets different needs. It may be a time to reduce financial stress by moving to less expensive quarters and preserving capital.

Stay productive. Many retired executives have found that enrolling in volunteer organizations provided new challenges and chances to contribute their skills and knowledge for meaningful results. It is difficult to suddenly retire when you have been productive most of your life. It is not only hard for you, but also for your partner and family.

Assess your life. Retirement is a valuable time to assess what you have accomplished in your life of work, how you have helped people, the contributions you have made to organizations and charities, the love and caring you have given to your family, and to realize you have made a difference.

Recognize when your powers are failing. A bassoonist in a major symphony orchestra told us that he began to hear a loss of quality in his playing. He decided to quit the orchestra rather than become a poor performer, and was able to find employment and use some organizational skills he had acquired over the years. He knew it was time to quit. Events and time will lead naturally to an end of formal work.

Stay active. You'll be in good stead if you have other interests besides work or work interests to pursue. Your worst enemy is idleness after a life of activity. Do something, even if you don't have a job, preferably something you feel is important. Keep active, exercise and watch your diet, so you can have a healthy life. Hopefully, you'll be lucky enough to have a career where your interests can be pursued, even if you are no longer actively employed.

Better still, it would be wise to have sufficient funds set aside to cover your expenses for a six month period as well as retirement. It is a good idea, even if you're not retired, to provide for contingencies with minimal stress. This will give you freedom to make choices at difficult times, instead of having to take the first job that presents itself or stay with a particular job that is distasteful and unrewarding, or to make hasty decisions.

Continue relationships. Even though you've retired, keep in touch with treasured colleagues and clients. In addition to the warmth of social contact, you may find opportunities to use your knowledge and experience to provide some help and counseling, to heighten your sense of being a valuable person. Attending professional meetings and adding to your knowledge are other ways you can feel more alive.

Summary

Having read this chapter, you now know that when you are emotionally healthy in your job, business or career, the following conditions are possible:

- Enjoyment in your work
- Doing the best that can be done and taking pride in doing things well
- Improving your skills for self-development
- Having a set of goals that advance your trade or career
- Compatibility with partners, colleagues and bosses
- Discussing feelings and issues openly with others and working on issues with an eye toward win-win solutions
- Understanding the practical realities and limitations of work

situations and either accepting them or changing work

- Being proactive rather than reactive in your own business and in organizations
- Being able to make a change rather than moping about the past
- Being able to adjust your financial habits if your are experiencing adverse circumstances
- Being able to quit when you're no longer able to function well
- Preparing for retirement and keeping your interests alive.

Chapter 7
Health

Do you have a lifelong commitment to your health? Or do you regard your health as a hit-or-miss affair, taking your chances and paying attention only as much as you need to "get by?"

Although your general health is influenced by your genes and also by the circumstances of your birth and upbringing, the possibilities available to you for enjoying a long and healthy life are greater than you might imagine. In this chapter, we will explore possibilities for staying healthy and active now and into your later years, physically, emotionally and sexually. But first, take the following quiz to examine your current status on the important matter of your physical health.

A Personal Assessment

Answer the following questions here or in your journal before reading this chapter, and then review after you have made any of the changes that are suggested.

1. On a scale from 1 to 10, rate your overall state of health: _____

2. Are you dealing with any major illnesses or other health issues at this time? _____

3. If so, list them here:

   _____

   _____

4. How often do you have medical checkups?

   _____

5. Do you always follow your doctor's recommendations (regimens, prescriptions, etc.)? _____

6. Do you get regular exercise? _____
   How often? _____

7. Do you pay attention to your diet and eat mostly healthy foods? _____

8. Rate how healthy your diet is on a scale of 1-10: _____

9. Are you currently overweight? _____
   If so, by how many pounds? _____

10. Do you have an end-of-life will? _____

Influences in Early Life

There are many influences in early life, both positive and negative, that shape your attitudes and behavior concerning your health. Many of these are learned and set during your childhood years. In terms of what we two octogenarians know now, so many of the experiences we had as children were not beneficial for our health. That hindsight prompted us to offer our children a better start than we got on developing life habits that lead to healthy living in adult years.

Take a moment to think about your own early years. What was your childhood like? Did you have a series of diseases, including whooping cough, scarlet fever, severe colds, bronchitis, infantile paralysis (polio), chicken pox, mumps or measles? Are there any residual effects? In Allan's case, Scarlett fever as a child affected his eyesight and led to wearing glasses. You, too, may have experienced a childhood illness the effects of which still are impacting your health today.

How about your diet? Did you have enough to eat as a child, or too much or too little? What kinds of foods did you eat—those that were sugar-laden, fatty and high in carbohydrates, or those that were balanced nutritionally? As you have seen in the many news stories about obesity, many of us got the wrong start, unwittingly, at the family table or in our snacking habits.

Examples of poor eating in early childhood habits abound. A friend told us his mother often said, *If you eat your spinach, you can have a double portion of French fries.* We're sure she had good intentions, but our friend's resulting life-long craving for French fries didn't do him much good. Another mother would promise sweets as an incentive, bringing out a rich dessert or candy as a behavioral reward. If you were influenced in similar ways and find it hard to give up such "treats" as an adult, it is certainly understandable. Such habits become deeply ingrained.

There are other family values regarding health, in addition to those influencing eating habits, that shape your current attitudes. A scholar friend had her interest as a child in playing tennis derided at home, because her parents felt she should be studying and not wasting time on "stupid things," like sports. How about you? As a child, you may have been fairly active, participating in sports and playing games as most children do. If that experience was combined with more systematic training and carried on throughout your life, you probably enjoy good physical health today. However, if you became sedentary, more isolated and inactive, then you may have already begun to develop a loss of muscle tone, poor circulation, and declining coordination to plague you in your later years.

Early experiences with dentists, physicians, and other health care specialists may have been unpleasant, possibly painful, making periodic examinations something to be avoided—unless you believed you really needed a doctor. One woman recalled her childhood panic at being isolated in a hospital ward for a heart problem and watching the girl in the next bed die. Today, she panics whenever she has to go to a hospital for any kind of treatment. A successful attorney who is a fearless squash player cowers at going to the dentist, because his elementary school had provided free dentistry for poor children and he'd had the horrifying experience of undergoing drilling without anesthesia. Today, he delays going to the dentist's office as long as he can, because for him it is a place of terror.

Friends weren't always helpful in fostering good health habits either, especially during adolescence. At one time, when smoking was more in vogue, it was a thrill to light up a cigarette and act like the more mature members of the group. But doing so also meant you began a highly addictive habit that is known for its detrimental health consequences. Alcohol, too, may have been a substance first tasted for the thrill of group acceptance and then became lethal later, especially when combined with driving. In later years, you may have gotten involved with drugs as part of your particular group's search for ecstasy and excitement, another negative factor for your enduring health.

Certainly mass media advertising hasn't helped any of us, sending out a constant stream of pictures of luscious hamburgers, pizzas, cookies and candies into our awareness. These unhealthy "junk foods" seem to be offered endlessly as tasty treats, frequently shown associated with people all having a good time. The encouragement for adding pounds starts early and bombards us every day with its appeal to eat more, promising happiness if we do. In addition, they use extra-thin models, further compounding and confusing the message.

While childhood and adolescence can be dangerous grounds for future health habits, adult life doesn't always favor the necessary discipline to maintain health, either. You may work long hours, find it difficult or awkward to take time to exercise, feel too tired, watch a lot of TV with snacks, and get distracted by all the family matters you have to take care of. Exercise and conscious dieting may be totally unappealing, occurring like deprivations that rob you of precious moments to relax, enjoy yourself, or have some fun.

Our point is that you have to go against the grain if you want to live a healthful life, and this can be challenging. If you've been lucky and have friends whose normal behavior follows healthy guidelines, you're more likely to succeed. Indeed, social factors can play an important role in stimulating beneficial behavior, for example joining a club that offers membership in a gym or associating with a group that prefers health foods when dining out. Having a spouse or partner who keeps you honest in this regard can be a blessing, even though you may find the support unpleasant when it occurs as nagging.

Regardless of the habits you may have picked up from activities and associations in earlier years, in this chapter, we will identify and explore possibilities that are available to help you maintain a positive state of health for many years to come.

Take a Measure of Your Health

As a point of reference for our discussion of health, it is essential to describe the characteristics of a physically healthy person. Indeed, such a description can become the yardstick by which you measure just how healthy—or unhealthy—you have become.

First, obviously, is the absence of malignancies, coronary diseases, diabetes, strokes and other illnesses. As a healthy person, you wouldn't be experiencing unusual pains, such as chronic headaches, digestive problems, unusual fatigue, or inability to sleep. There would be few instances of major dental problems, muscle or joint pains, or other signs of serious deterioration. Occasional instances of these conditions do not indicate ill-health but are to be expected at certain times during life. Also, some disabilities can be genetic, such as birth defects, resulting in loss of one or more limbs, while a person can be completely healthy in other respects.

A second measure of being physically healthy is the presence of an emotionally healthy attitude. Indeed, the body and mind aren't separate but have been shown by science to continuously interact. You are a psychosomatic unit, meaning *psyche* and *soma*, mind and body, are connected. If you are emotionally healthy, you are interested in using your mind to stay aware of your body and your general well-being; you value your state of health and want to do whatever is essential for maintaining a positive state. You assume responsibility for periodic checkups and remedies, and generally make lifestyle choices that promote good health. You realize that bodily health can affect general emotional health, and that problems in your emotional life can affect your physical health.

As aging occurs, emotionally healthy people accept changes and limitations without becoming depressed and non-functioning. You would seek alternatives when first choices can't be used. You would naturally have an interest in learning about what is going to keep you healthy and take steps to ensure that your health be maintained.

Let's not forget the terrible effect of pain and intense discomfort on attitude, humor and behavior when you are seriously ill. When you're sick, you don't have energy to deal with even the smallest challenges, making you highly irritable and sometimes oblivious to what else is going on. There is a very serious price to pay when pain is continuous and intense, which is all the more reason to avoid the consequences that can occur when you fail to maintain good health.

When you are emotionally healthy, you naturally take responsibility for yourself and your health by choosing possible avenues that will support your continued well-being. Below is a checklist of some of those possibilities for you to use in assessing your level of responsibility in regards to your health.

As an emotionally healthy person you would:

- Have annual physicals and periodic checkups. Your medical support team, depending on your gender, should include an internist, a cardiologist, a dermatologist, a urologist, a gynecologist, and others as needed.
- Follow prescriptions and recommendations made for changing your behavior.
- Exercise regularly and follow a healthy diet. This should be done not only for yourself, but to serve as a model for your children and others who live with you.
- Get all the help you can when you need it and accept what you get.
- Keep anxieties related to realities. A 1 per cent failure rate in a particular operation doesn't mean if you have it, you're going to die. A single skin cancer of the benign type doesn't mean you're doomed.
- Learn to live with chronic conditions gracefully and without complaint.
- Avoid toxic substances like tobacco, excessive alcohol, and drugs.

When you're young and healthy, choosing such possibilities as those described above may seem impractical, even obsessive. You also may be anxious to avoid the costs of such extensive care. However, as you age, you will want to increase the frequency of these positive behaviors to prevent potentially dangerous factors from impacting your life permanently.

Health and Aging

If you, like us, are looking back on a lifetime of experiences regarding your health and well-being, there may be some regrets. You may have been athletic and always enjoyed walking in the countryside, playing competitive games like tennis, and feeling vigorous. Now you have difficulty walking, your balance is unsteady, your breathing after most activities difficulties labored, and you can't seem to muster the energy that you used to have. It can be depressing to think that all you can look forward to are more debilitating moments.

Are there ways in which this decline could have been prevented or ameliorated? Can you still find meaningful things to do and enjoy, in spite of your declining health status?

Even though you know what it takes to be healthy and avoid illness, there comes a time when your body naturally begins to change or weaken. Failing eyesight and hearing, balance problems, cardiovascular threats, menopause, back pains, difficulty in walking, prostate problems, and endocrinal changes are all possible problems that you can experience when aging.

Therefore, as you age, you have to become more diligent in listening to your body. It is especially valuable to make lifestyle changes earlier rather than later in order to minimize the decline in your physical flexibility and health. By doing so, you can maintain strength and flexibility into your later years.

Here's where emotional factors have an especially important effect. You may not wish to make changes out of reluctance to acknowledge your loss of functioning or potential decline. You may simply feel too threatened about what it might imply. Women experiencing endocrinal changes may become irritable and easily upset or depressed. They may especially feel their changing appearance will make them less attractive and loveable, and that mood alterations may affect their ability to take care of their families. Concerns about appearance also affect men—consider all the advertisements for treatment of baldness and sexual dysfunction.

Regardless of the many emotional deterrents to doing what it takes to stay fit and healthy, maintaining a healthy regime from early years can be empowering.

Getting Older But Not "Getting Old"

A friend of Irv's was describing his decision to sell his condo and move to a retirement home. The man was a successful attorney whose wife had died 20 years ago, with children who had, in turn, substantial career success. He had decided to stop everything he was doing and prepare for his final days, despite being in good health. When Irv talked about his own dental practice, his various projects including writing, the attorney replied, "Irv, you're getting older, but I'm *getting old.*"

Too many people equate *older* with *old*. *Getting old* means that as they age, they fail to sustain interests, stop learning, and adopt a passive role with regard to children in their lives. In short, they begin to die before their time, even when still young. *Getting older* implies there are always new possibilities for action and involvement in all phases of life, such as meeting new people, sharing experiences and pursuing interests. Being alive means taking a vital interest in life and seeking out new possibilities for satisfaction. If you're not doing this, you'll most likely fall in line with Irv's friend and *get old*, not simply *older* as you age.

What You Should Watch For

As you age, it's important to be observant and pay attention to health conditions that are to be expected. Partners can also be helpful to each other in spotting conditions potentially leading to illness and alert one another as to their existence. They can call attention to:

- Loss of memory
- Failing eyesight
- Balance problems (Falling can lead to hip problems and even death)
- Hearing loss
- Increased blood pressure
- Large weight loss or gain (unplanned)
- Eating foods that have a high cholesterol value
- Suspicious lumps or malignancies of the skin or breast
- Chronic constipation or diarrhea
- Back pains
- Digestive disturbances

Attitudes and Illness

Attitude can make a huge difference in how people respond to their aging and illness. Two contrasting examples demonstrate this.

An 85-year-old woman who, when getting out of bed, fell and fractured her hips and wrist. She recovered but resisted using a wheelchair. This was especially problematic when she had to go outside. Her reason was that she didn't want her neighbors to see her and think she was too old and decrepit! Her vanity kept her at risk for another injury, while her neighbors were spared their possible judgments.

A 75-year-old man had severe back trouble that limited his ability to be upright and mobile. A former home builder, he felt inadequate and helpless, until he realized he could still put his skills to work by having his house reconstructed. First, he purchased a wheelchair with a number of controls. Next, he had all the counters lowered, so he could reach them and placed hand bars at key places around the house for assistance getting in and out of the wheelchair. He bought a computer that accepted verbal instructions, so he doesn't have to sit for a long time while using it. Since it is difficult for him to visit friends, he schedules computer talks.

Note the difference between a passive attitude—the 85-year-old woman—and a pro-active attitude—the 75-year-old man—and the effect of their different attitudes on the possibilities for positive outcomes.

Your attitude can impact your health at any age, as the above two examples clearly show. Here is a list of negative attitudes you want to avoid as you age in order to have optimal health:

- Pride—you don't want to appear old and fragile.

- Isolating yourself—you are afraid to rely on others.

- Guilt—you feel bad for being dependent on others.

- Fear—you don't want to acknowledge the inevitable.

- Denial—you refuse to acknowledge the inevitable. "I'm not *really* sick."

Elisabeth Kubler-Ross is a psychoanalyst and author who wrote *On Death and Dying*, a book about the last stages of life. In it, she describes five stages that are not only typical of events during terminal illness, but also of emotional stages people go through before they accept death. These are:

1. Denial—you insist that there is nothing wrong.
2. Blame—you find fault with others for your problems. "The doctor should have caught this earlier." "If only people had reminded me of the importance of diet!"
3. Self-Blame—you blame yourself. "This is happening to me because I wasn't a good person." "This is what I deserve for not having paid attention to my body."
4. Acceptance—you recognize that you are sick, may be going to die, and you'd like to make plans for how to deal with it.

The first three stages are natural defenses against any perceived threat, but once the fourth one, acceptance, has taken place, there is the possibility of problem solving that can help to achieve a more satisfactory ending.

Personality Types and Attitudes

Another factor in how people respond to aging and illness relates to the four personality types previously mentioned in Chapter 5 Financial Security: 1) idealistic yet passive, 2) independent and active, 3) planned and deliberate, and 4) friendly and adaptive. See if you can recognize yourself in the following descriptions. These types can be seen in typical responses to illness as well as financial situations.

The first type, the *passive idealist*, reacts to illness with dependency and guilt. You are willing to accept treatment and care but not willing to take any initiative regarding that treatment, unless especially encouraged and helped.

The *independent active* type likes to be in control of what is happening. If you can characterize your behavior in this way, you become highly frustrated and angry when things don't go well, in some cases becoming blaming and aggressive. In such distressful circumstances, you can't stand delays and respond poorly to bodily failings that impede activity. However, you may try to find solutions on your own.

The *deliberate thoughtful* type needs everything to be planned and to follow a logical progression of events. You want to know what is happening and get upset by changes in the routine, failure to follow the usual sequences, or emergencies that arise. You have a tendency to be serious and withdrawn in illness, lacking a sense of humor and not responding to jokes.

Finally, there is the *friendly adaptive* type. You are inclined to be a more socially related person who tends to respond to illness by making friends with the health providers, joking about conditions, and being willing to change when requested or needed. You try to make the best of the situation, and are outgoing and hearty, expecting a friendly greeting whenever you meet someone. However, you likely have an intense concern about illnesses that affect your appearance or create negative conditions in your relationships.

What is your pattern? How you respond to the same conditions as another person depends on your personality. If this is recognized by health care providers, and they are flexible in how they provide treatment to accommodate the different types, it is easier to accept their help. For example, if a nurse in a hospital recognizes you as a deliberate and thoughtful type who needs a logical explanation for any changes in routine, she may be more willing to give you the detailed answers you need to quell your anxiety and discomfort.

Sexuality, Aging and Health

An important topic for lifelong health is sexual behavior and attitudes, especially as we change with age. In the natural course of aging, we move from passion to routine encounters, and sometimes to disinterest or even resentment.

The topic of sexuality and aging is seldom discussed by the people who are affected. As we indicated in Chapter 3 in our discussion of intimate relationships, sexual experience is usually not fully and freely faced by couples at the outset of their relationship, often leading to a breakdown in their level of satisfaction. An emotionally healthy approach, however, would be for couples to admit any difficulties and strive for some problem solving.

Let's examine the facts about sexual health in aging and then look more closely at what it means to have an emotionally healthy attitude about sexuality.

Aging can bring some natural physical changes that have an impact on your sexual behavior and attitudes. As a man, you may experience a decline in sexual interest due to lower levels of the male sexual hormone, testosterone. Other health factors that can affect both men and women's ability to partake fully in sexual activities as they age are diabetes, urinary problems, heart maladies, menopause, endocrinal changes, and painful ailments affecting bodily movement.

Medication used in treating health problems, such as antihypertensive drugs, the use of Flomax and Proscar for an enlarged prostate, surgical interventions, and hormonal injections, can all produce additional problems. Among these problems for men are erection difficulties, reduced libido, decreased semen production, reverse ejaculation, as well as impotency. For women, drugs and surgery can lead to emotional moodiness and affect sexual desire, as well as cause difficulty in achieving orgasm.

As a result, a variety of emotions are generated, as summarized in the following chart:

Responses to Changing Sexuality

Men may feel:	Women may feel:
Impotent	Less interest in sex
Depressed	Responsible for men's failures
Less masculine	Less feminine
Sexually inadequate	Sexually inadequate

Frustrated and resentful   Frustrated and resentful

Inadequate as a person   Inadequate as a person

Emotionally Healthy Sexuality

Sexual relations are an important part of relationships in most cultures. Unfortunately, we tend to regard sexual relations as more serious when things are not as they are expected to be, regardless of how satisfied a couple may feel about their general state of affairs, the family, compatibility, or finances. Such matters as erections and orgasms often dominate the fantasies and affect how partners evaluate their relationships, creating intense psychological discomfort for many.

Adding to the problem, men often feel their capability in life is measured by their sexual prowess. This is especially true during adolescence, when the number of sexual experiences lend prestige to the person who claims them. Those who don't have such experiences often feel inferior to those who do. Other males boast about the quality of their experiences, causing grown men to come to their partners feeling required to perform at high levels and experience fantastic peaks of excitement. Such expectations are so "real," that it becomes the way couples measure success in their relationship. Men even expect that every sexual encounter should be highly orgasmic and that their partners should experience high satisfaction and express it afterwards.

For women, sex is often highly associated with romance and caring, although women can be as interested in sheer sexual enjoyment as men, despite the fact that most cultures tend to minimize such a possibility. Expectations of satisfaction are also high for women, and a failure to achieve orgasm may have implications of inadequacy, as well as create frustration for their mates.

But you have to ask: Are these expectations a good basis to measure emotional health in regards to sexuality? We believe a different approach to measuring emotional health has to be taken, one that regards sexual engagement as more than a mainly physical encounter including erection, penetration and orgasm. Rather, it is essential to see sex as part of the total ongoing nature of two people being together, integrated into the fabric of their shared lives. Just as in other areas of life as you age, realize problems exist and try to understand each other's experience and capabilities. You need to behave in similar ways in the area of sexuality, if emotional health is to be demonstrated.

When Sex Is a Problem

When sexual problems arise, it's wise to be open and discuss what is happening with your partner. Partners seldom talk about the quality of their experience, but this is an important topic of any discussion. You want your partner to think the experience was great for you, but what if it wasn't? Do you share openly about what each does to turn on and off the other? Such frankness and honesty requires recognition of inadequacies, acceptance, and a commitment to solving problems. It also requires you to be open to suggestions for increasing yours and your partner's satisfaction and pleasure. Make agreements to try different behaviors that will increase gratification.

As you age, remember: All sex doesn't have to rely on erections and penetration. Exploring other avenues can allow for much gratification. Oral and tactual sex may be quite satisfactory. Sometimes the use of dildos can be useful. Be inventive and come up with some other ways to provide sexual joy and release if the more traditional channels are not available due to health conditions.

We recall a TV interview with the movie star Christopher Reeves and his wife, before he died. The former "Superman" was completely paralyzed from the neck down due to an accident while horseback riding on a set, yet when the interviewer asked them about their marital relationship, they both lit up and unabashedly confided that sexual activity could take alternative forms for people as much in love as they were.

Above all, don't chide or make fun of the other person for any aging deficiencies they may be experiencing—although it doesn't hurt to have a sense of humor about declining abilities! Be sensitive to your partner, and enjoy the relationship and the love.

And finally, don't forget about expressing your sincere care and interest in the other person. Interest in the other only as a sex object will diminish the interest of the other party in sex faster than anything.

Your Doctor and Your Health

When some people fall ill and must visit a doctor, they are reluctant to tell their doctor everything about their health conditions. There are many reasons for such reluctance, possibly because they want the doctor to like them and don't want to be too much of a burden. There is also consideration for the doctor's time and the fear of being charged too much if they provide lengthy descriptions. Some people don't want to be told that they are seriously ill, a concern that prevents them from fully disclosing everything to their doctor about their health.

If you are someone who wants the best medical help, however, it is essential to disclose as much about your illness as possible. Just mentioning a fleeting pain in another area than that being examined may provide a critical diagnostic clue to your physician. Hopefully, your doctor will listen to you fully and note what you are saying. (If he or she doesn't, see our next section for finding a doctor that does.)

Equally important in your disclosure is a list of all the medications and their strengths that you are currently taking, along with all the supplements you take on your own. You may have been convinced of the value of some supplement by an advertisement or a bulletin, but a supplement often requires something else to make it work, as in the case of Calcium which needs Vitamin D to help in its absorption. The reason to disclose such information to your doctor is that some supplements will interfere with your medications. If your doctor doesn't know about what else you are taking, mistakes in prescriptions can occur that may be detrimental to your health.

If symptoms change at any time—an ache disappears, another becomes more intense or additional pains seem to emerge—your doctor should be informed. Some patients with chronic illnesses find it convenient to keep a daily log of symptoms and their severity, which can be helpful when describing your condition to your doctor.

Being Proactive With Your Doctor

We have emphasized the importance of periodic medical examinations as a way you can help your doctor help you, but now we must call attention to another aspect of the doctor-patient relationship. That is to encourage you to be proactive in all your communications. Too many patients are passive, meaning they accept what their doctor tells them, and fail to question and comment on his remarks.

There can be dire consequences when you fail to be proactive. We heard this story: A doctor told his patient to increase a prescription dosage despite the fact that the last change had made him extremely fatigued and dizzy. After taking the prescription, the patient went into a coma and had to be hospitalized.

Whenever your doctor suggests a change in medication, ask him for the reason. If you have had bad effects from one type of medication, remind your doctor about it. You may want to carry with you a complete list of medications you are taking when you visit your doctor's office. Even though your physician may have those medications in his files, he may not pay full attention to them due to a heavy patient load that caused him to forget.

Be proactive and speak up when you have questions. If your doctor orders a test, ask him about the purpose of the test and what changes he will make depending upon the results. If nothing will be done as a result of the tests, refuse to take them. Beware of overly routine tests that may not be useful. It appears that PSA for prostate cancer tests, for example, may not be useful and actually lead to a large number of falsely positive results. Frequent mammograms may be harmful because of the excessive radiation. Often tests are used to protect the doctor in case of a mistake he might make in diagnosis, and may not even be needed by the unsuspecting patient.

If your doctor fails to answer your questions or behaves in any way that you find unacceptable, let him know how you feel and how you want to be treated. One case we know about is as follows: A patient who was very ill was seen by her physician and told she should report any change in her symptoms. When her symptoms became worse, she called the physician, only to be told by his office that he wasn't in. When she said she would like to leave a message, the office told her that the doctor didn't normally call in for messages, although she was free to leave one. The woman tried to call her doctor three more times before deciding this doctor wasn't the one she cared to have any longer. Such behavior by any physician is unprofessional and could be serious enough to lead to a malpractice suit.

We repeat: If a doctor doesn't listen to you, even if you have reminded him about it, *change doctors.*

There are other grievances you should never let pass by. Doctors may relay information that is devastating to you and not realize how much you need to have additional information and comfort. We know of one incident in which a woman was informed she might have cancer, yet the doctor's next appointment was a month later. She was told he was unavailable for additional consultation before then. In another instance, a woman, feeling terribly cold in an office, asked the doctor if she could have a blanket. His reply was, "What do you think this is, a hotel?" There is no excuse for such an utterly insensitive response, yet it is allowed by so many patients.

So often, patients are anxious, weak and dependent, and may be taking abuse as well as misunderstanding what they are being told. If you are somewhat dependent, try to bring another person along with you to your visits who can be your advocate and ask questions to make sure you are being treated properly.

In one instance, a patient in a hospital bed was receiving intravenous fluids when his visitor, who also happened to be a nurse, noticed that the drip was not adjusted properly. The visitor promptly called attention to the error and it was corrected. Sometimes the doctor may not know (although he should) how patients are being treated by his staff, and so it is helpful for patients or their advocates to speak up when they see mistreatment of any kind.

If you feel mistreated by attendants, don't hesitate to let your doctor know about it. It is the doctor's responsibility to see to it that his staff are trained to exhibit proper behavior. An example of such mistreatment is a diabetic patient who was served a meal in a hospital that was not only heavily laden with carbohydrates but also included a piece of cake iced with a rich sugar frosting. Fortunately, a relative was present who insisted that the inappropriate food be removed and a meal suitable for a diabetic diet be served instead.

Sometimes you are given the run-around. Your own doctor referred you to see a senior physician who is a specialist at another office, but when you get there, you never see that specialist. Instead, you are assigned to a junior member of the team who repeats basic procedures that have already been done and documented. If this happens, regardless of the senior doctor's time constraints or overloaded schedule, complain and refuse such treatment! You can always reschedule and request a time when the specialist referred by your doctor is available to see you.

In the case of serious illness when surgery is indicated, a good idea is to get at least one other consultation before making a decision. Obviously, emergency situations may not allow such a delay, but it is good policy whenever possible.

Health-care provider induced deaths have been on the rise for some time now, so it behooves us all to take extra care and not fall into the lull of false security that the doctor always knows best. Be on the alert and take responsibility for the choices that are made by interjecting your questions and requests.

On the other hand, if you have a doctor who listens to you, tries to answer your questions, follows up on your tests with a phone call or letter to discuss the results and is tactful in his remarks, lets you know when he doesn't have an answer, and refers you to specialist when needed, then treasure that doctor for the service provided. This is the behavior you have every right to receive as a patient. And don't forget to compliment and praise your doctor and staff when treatment is outstanding. Be sure and do all that you can to have your relationship with your physician prosper.

End of Life Health

Too often, the last years of life (usually somewhere between the 70s and 90s) present difficulties that require special help from family or nursing aides. Assistance may be needed to provide meals, pay attention to medicine/drug dosages, arrange for medical care, hospital and nursing care when needed, and transportation.

If you are ambulatory and can take care of yourself, it may still pay to have someone check on you periodically. You may even want to have either a partner or family member live with you. If you can afford it, you may want to have a part or full-time caretaker to assist in some life areas. Ideally, this would mean you have to experience few restrictions, save those imposed by awkward movements.

If you are non-ambulatory and need help on a 24 hour basis, you can either live at home, assuming there is someone attentive to your needs, or move to a private facility with nursing and medical care. Living in a senior facility with a medical center can provide a fuller life with opportunities for making friends, entertainment, transportation to stores and museums, as well as provide some medical aid if needed. Such an arrangement can be quite expensive, so it's good to have insurance for this eventuality, although there is government help available if you qualify. Before deciding to move to any facility, however, always have someone check it out to assure that good care is provided.

Hospice care—either at a center or in your home—is for the final days when special nursing care is needed. The staff is trained to understand the psychological needs of patients and can do much to provide comfort and sensitive care.

Emotionally healthy seniors are able both to accept help graciously, not grudgingly, and to express appreciation for such assistance. You have to remember that when you are in such a state, there is a heavy burden on others, and you should refrain from expressing irritation when your needs are not immediately attended to. However, there are personality types who, in response to illness and dying, can make it especially difficult, such as high control types who are frightened of anything that affects their independence, or passive types who may be reluctant to be a burden to anyone and therefore don't cooperate or act from guilt.

When quality of life deteriorates and becomes so diminished that you are barely aware of what is happening, it is important to have a living will that guarantees the end will not be preceded by heroic attempts to keep the barest spark alive. In the book, *Tuesdays with Morrie*, Morrie decided to live until he could no longer wipe his own backside. Others may have different criteria for their decisions. Certainly, it is not something that can be decided by anyone else. What might be unacceptable to someone as a condition for continuing life might be perfectly fine to another who is clinging to life as long as possible. Our point is: Let the people around you know what you want as a necessary condition for continuing your life, and get it written down in a living will.

Parting Thoughts

When people feel their existence is terminal, they naturally want to give treasured items to those they love. Rather than protesting or saying it is premature, accept the gifts with gratitude so the person giving them can have the blessing of feeling appreciated in their final moments. It is also a way of continuing to remember. Many elderly people would like to discuss plans for their ending—listen intently, so they don't feel ignored. When possible, arrange the opportunity to say goodbye in a loving way.

It's not always easy to accept the departure of someone you love, regardless of their age. A child who was dying was visited by a counselor and asked what could be done to help him. He asked that counseling be provided to his family, since they refused to accept the idea of his death.

It would be helpful if anxieties could be discussed openly and people could take the time to make the final departure meaningful, to share their loving thoughts, special memories and their anxieties, as well. In short, the openness that we recommend for other areas of life works for this period of life, as well.

Summary

- Good health means taking care of yourself with periodic examinations.
- Good health also means following a schedule that includes proper diet, exercise and cultivating positive emotional attitudes.
- Emotions can affect health and vice versa—when observing health, look for changes in both areas.
- Learn to accept changes and change accordingly.
- When making changes, start with small ones—e.g. start with 10 minutes worth of exercise or try to lose 5 pounds in a month. Then make a commitment to maintain the change.
- Be proactive in dealing with your doctor, as well as other care-givers and institutions.
- Be open to discussing issues of health and sexual behavior.
- Plan for your final days.

Part III
Moving Forward

Chapter 8
Stress and Distress

You can't understand it: Where once you were confident, on top of the world, you now are uncertain and fraught with self-doubt. Your heart pounds like crazy when you are the slightest bit apprehensive. There are moments of dread that cause you to forget everything else, and you obsess over every little criticism that comes your way. At times, you wonder where the fun in life went and after many a restless night, greet each day as another chapter in a very boring routine.

How did you get to this highly stressed state, and what could you have done to prevent it? In this chapter, you'll have a chance to explore some choices in life that don't take you down the road to more and more stress. We offer many suggestions for how to deal with and even prevent the anxiety, dread and depression that accompany stressful episodes in life, all responses that put you into the state of *dis-stress*.

A Personal Assessment

Review your experience of the stress in your life by answering the following questions either by writing in your journal or in the spaces provided:

1. On a scale from 1 to 10, indicate how stressful your life is currently: _____

2. Which of the following areas of life cause you the most distress? Underline your choice or choices, and then write any incidents that come to mind you are dealing with currently:

   a. Intimate Relations

   _____

   b. Parenting

   _____

   c. Financial Security

   _____

   d. Work

   _____

   e. Health

   _____

3. On a scale from 1 to 10, assess how much your involvement in and reaction to the incidents you've identified contribute to your experience: _____

4. List at least three things that you could do to relieve your distress:

   _____

   _____

   _____

5. Name one more thing that you could do to relieve your distress:

   _____

Responding to Stress

Stress affects us all—no one escapes the pressures of modern life. Yet we know that, to paraphrase an old saying, *different folks suffer from different strokes*. What is devastating to one person may not bother another, even though some events may overwhelm us all.

Some of the differences in how people respond to stress are due to genetic origins. Psychologists studied infant reactions and discovered three types of responders: *internalizers*, *externalizers* and *generalizers*. Infants categorized as internalizers showed very little external reaction to stress, but measurements of heart rate and hormonal secretions showed they were having intense internal reactions. Externalizers showed their reactions by activity, such as crying and other agitations, while generalizers had both kinds of reactions. On follow up, some of these patterns continued throughout life, determining how a person might respond to difficult or stressful situations. In addition to these infant studies, other studies of people with bi-polar disorder have shown significant emotional pattern differences at birth.

Some stress response differences are well-known and have been codified in relation to research done on the causes of heart attacks. Two personality types were identified, Type A and Type B, each characterizing distinctive patterns of behavior, with Type As being more prone to cardiac failure than Type Bs. Type A personalities tend to be high-achieving, driven people who pay the price of heart health from over-striving.

Strangely enough, the very strengths, attitudes and values that underlie our successes also create our stressed feelings when they are over used in uncomfortable, threatening and risky situations. Those strengths, such as the relentless drive of the Type A personality, eventually predispose us to difficulties in managing life and may even lead to subsequent illness. Yet their very presence gives us the key to mastering stress in our lives.

As adults, we are faced with the fact that we differ from others in how we react to stressful stimuli. Yet taking this into consideration, we still need to control our external and internal responses before they become excessive and destructive. This may require the help of others or such techniques as forcing ourselves to stop, reassessing a situation, and considering other possibilities. Learning stress-reduction techniques such as meditation may also help.

Distress—A Kind of Stress

Before we discuss possible effective techniques, let us clarify some terms. Dr. Hans Selye, a pioneer in stress research, defined two kinds of stress. One is related to challenge and opportunities, which he called *stress*, while another is related to extremely intense experiences that are precipitated by threats, which he called *distress*. Stress can therefore be thought of as essential for coping with life experiences, and the more threatening form, distress, refers to stress that can be overwhelming and problematic. In this book, we use the term *distress* to refer to the latter.

A life without stress—challenge and opportunities—would be boring. There would be almost no incentive to live. This is because we usually respond to stress with increased energy and creative problem-solving. Indeed, there are some people who seek the experience of stress as peak moments in their lives, for example, a mountain climber or participant in any extreme sport.

The experience of distress, on the other hand, often triggers intense emotional responses and can often blind you to the possibilities that exist, forcing you to see things from only one limited view. In addition, emotionally distressing states are not only unpleasant in themselves, but they, in turn, can cause health problems. In this book, we have shown how distress is caused by breakdowns in the five areas of life we have discussed and then considered possible ways of coping with them.

Sources of Your Distress

The sources for distress are highly individual, even though some kinds of *distressors* (the stimuli that cause distress) might be universal, such as someone coming at you with a knife raised to strike. In some instances, reactions such as increased blood flow, increased levels of adrenalin, and muscular behavior are almost automatic whenever there is a perceived threat. Some of us react to the threat as long as it lasts and then recover by returning to our normal functioning. Others may continue to be stimulated by thoughts of the threat, their bodies reacting as if the threat were still happening, leading ultimately to malfunctions and illness. Ulcers, heart problems, rashes, even back problems may be related to such chronic responses to stress.

Some sources of distress are common to all of us, the most predominant being abrupt or significant changes in our life circumstances. In the U.S. the three most common sources of distress for people are changes in marital status, changes in job, and moving to a new location.

The following are other sources of distress:

- Negative evaluations of a situation or experience
- Frustrations that prevent desired outcomes
- Too many demands in a short period of time –
  or constant heavy loads.
- Loss of resources
- Invasion of territory (physical and psychological)
- Threats to loved ones
- Lack of support (physical and psychological)
- Betrayal and deceit
- Anger experienced from another
- Life threats (including severe illness)

In each of the five areas of life covered in this book's discussion—intimate relations, parenting, financial security, work, and health—events occur that are sources of both stress and distress. In the previous chapters, we examined the sources and effects of distressing events in life, and offered possibilities for alternate behaviors and attitudes. In this chapter, we will integrate that material into a more general framework and give you tips for preventing and managing distress in your life.

Coping Styles for Managing Distress

People cope with distress in unique and individual styles, each style fitting a predictable pattern of response. Below we have described four such coping styles that you may recognize in yourself or in others. While these are not the only possible styles, they are fairly common ones showing how people react to distress, as well as the particular distress-ful experiences that cause the most severe problems.

Submissive-Receptive style. Whenever experiencing distress, this person feels overwhelmed, unable to cope, and pessimistic about outcomes. Such feelings may be attributed to bad luck, lack of skills, or a history of unfortunate experiences. In addition, the person often experiences guilt for the events that have occurred, as if he or she is to blame for all that has happened. Fortunately, this person also feels dependent and is likely to be receptive to suggestions, especially when coming from someone perceived as capable and wise who doesn't blame them.

Controlling-Persistent style. This person often feels capable of handling a stressful situation but gets frustrated when what has been successful no longer works. There will be a tendency to persist, taking actions even when such actions are not working. There is also reluctance to ask for help, unless it is quite clear that the situation involves competencies the person does not possess. It is difficult for this person to allow someone to completely take over, responding better when shown what to do and then entrusted to take charge personally.

Cautious-Resistant style. Characteristically, such a person relies on rules, structures and known procedures to solve problems. There is a tendency to approach situations slowly, spend time understanding what is involved, and pay attention to every detail. Disruption of routines, schedules and habits can be very threatening. Rapid change causes difficulties, and emergencies that require immediate response may be deferred until they become overwhelming. Accepting help is difficult, unless clearly explained and demonstrated. There will be a strong tendency to persist in what is known rather than to readily appraise the situation and adapt accordingly. This person also has difficulty handling emotions; indeed, he or she strives to remove emotions from consideration and so may experience intense distress when emotions need to be resolved.

Flexible-Socially-Concerned style. Someone who emphasizes this style pays close attention to social factors when dealing with distressful situations. Other people's reactions are extremely important, so attention is placed on being able to read and understand people and being flexible in accommodating people and situations. The person generally has an optimistic attitude that persists even when experiencing high degrees of distress. "Everything will turn out all right!" is a typical remark. Until he or she is able to find a solution, there can be a constant trying out of possibilities, but with an impatience that may lead to many changes without solutions. A particular source of distress would be negative opinions and criticisms coming from others, often creating high states of anxiety. Much effort is spent on maintaining behavior that will be viewed as prestigious and acceptable to others. Excessive humor is one way this person responds to distress.

Do you recognize yourself in any of these patterns of response to distress? Which one fits the way you cope with distress in your life?

How Distress Affects Possibilities

When you are in poor health, experiencing a crisis, or under other severe circumstances, you are less likely to easily see possibilities for alternative solutions to your problems. This is because distress in general prepares the body for emergency types of responses by increasing alertness and sharpening focus. The accompanying preoccupation with self, along with feelings of depression and frustration when distress is keen, make you seek the familiar and secure rather than the unique or novel, and your access to solutions is thereby narrowed.

Consider the following examples of how distress alters the perception of possible solutions:

An associate was recently diagnosed with severe arthritis. She became increasingly restricted because of painful movements and was discouraged by medications that not only failed to ease her problems but added side effects of nausea and chronic fatigue. She has been urged to try more holistic approaches, even some highly publicized programs of nutrition and exercise, but she refuses to see them as viable possibilities, relying only on the advice provided by her general practitioner. "Why should I pay him, unless I follow what he prescribes?" is one of her favorite responses when questioned about trying alternative therapies for her condition.

Another person is an entrepreneur who created a small business that has more orders than he can handle. Since he is already in debt, he is unwilling to assume new debt that would enable him to add staff and expand manufacturing capacity. He can't see this solution as a possibility, so remains heavily burdened by working long hours under his current highly distressing situation, despite recommendations of friends and consultants.

A physician built a large practice and is constantly trying to enlarge it by participating in a wide range of social networks. This has caused him to work seven days a week, averaging twelve hour days, believing he should always be available for his patients. He has little time to spend at home with his wife and children who have become increasingly resentful of his practice. His wife is thinking about divorce, but he can't see how he can possibly reduce the number of hours he works, since, as he says, "I am building for my future!" He feels desperate but still resists offers to merge his practice with that of others. Further, he feels that his wife should understand his pressures and goals, since the result of his activity will benefit her and the children in the future.

We're sure that you, too, have experienced times when you felt painted into a corner, unable to see any possible way to solve a particular problem you are dealing with. What can you do when you're in such a state? How can you open your eyes and see that other possibilities do indeed exist?

While it is extremely difficult to do, the best thing you can do when you feel totally trapped by a dilemma in life is to take a mental vacation from the issue. Why does this work? As long as you feel trapped and believe there is no recourse, the distress will mount and limit your perception of a more helpful path. You'll never see your way out of the trap, unless you take a break from seeing yourself *in a trap*.

Exercise: Take a Mental Vacation

A helpful way we have found to respond to stressful situations is to take a "mental vacation." This involves leaving your usual approach of worrying or fretting about a situation and trying something different. One way is to imagine you are your own consultant. What questions would you ask your client (*you*) that would stimulate him or her to think outside of the box? Make a list of solutions that are "way out," completely outside of your comfort zone, and write them in your journal. Don't dismiss any of them. When you've finished your list, go back and see if you can identify what it would take to make just one of those possibilities a reality.

You may want to involve your partner or a good friend in this exercise, since it's often easier for someone who is not involved to see possibilities you cannot. Others can listen to your view of things and bring in a new experience that goes beyond your own.

Here's an example of how we do this: Irv is extremely knowledgeable about all kinds of financial matters, so Allan finds him a valuable resource when he experiences distress in financing a venture. Allan is extremely adept at finding what to say to people in difficult circumstances, so Irv uses him to test statements he might have to make in uncomfortable or risky situations. We repeat here a topic we mentioned earlier in this book: Know your own strengths and make use of others' strengths when you are weak in a particular area.

While attending a memorial service recently, we noted the temple had distributed a flyer to its members, on which was printed the message: *Embrace the possibilities!* How true!

Key Factors in Being Able to Handle Distress

There are several factors that can impact your ability to handle distress. Use the following checklist to evaluate if any of these factors are affecting you and what changes you can make.

1. *General tolerance and wellness.* This can be genetic factors,

physical health maintenance and care, including regular examinations, dieting, and timely interventions by professionals.

2. *Relaxation.* Know when to take breaks, preferably scheduled in advance.

3. *Exercise.* Schedule regular activities, preferably aerobic ones.

4. *Sleep.* Make sure you get enough, at least 6 hours per day

5. *Harmful habits.* Avoid overwork, addictions such as tobacco, alcohol, drugs, and worrying obsessively.

6. *Stamina.* Build your strength to withstand times of negative stress.

7. *Opportunities for venting.* Spend time with friends who will listen to you and be there for you. Avoid so-called friends who irritate you; they will only add to your distress. Use humor and try to find what is comical about your situation. Get other perspectives.

8. *Vacations, both real and imaginary.* By imaginary, we mean taking time away so you can remove yourself from the immediate distressful situation.

9. *Access to therapy and counseling.* When your choice of handling distress doesn't bring relief, outside help may be needed. Don't be one of those people who feel they ought to be able to handle everything life throws at them, failing to realize it's often impossible to do that.

10. *Willingness to change.* This can mean changing jobs, living location, hobbies, etc. An important motto to keep in mind

is: *Change what you can change and accept what you can't.*
The challenge, of course, is in knowing the difference!

Preparing for Change

Change—whether brought on by your own choice or seeming to come from out of nowhere—is often the main source of distress for people, so you want to be ready for changes before they overwhelm you. Following are some suggestions to help you prepare for making stressful changes.

Affirm your strengths and capabilities. It's important to think positively about yourself and to realize you can cope with situations.

Contract for change. Set schedules and evaluations. Change isn't easy because you're fighting a lifetime of habits. This is why you have to commit to it, evaluate what happens, and make corrections when needed.

Start small and expect some setbacks. Don't try to change everything at once. Choose small targets at first and build from success, but don't get discouraged.

Reward yourself for success. Rewards may be concrete, such as buying something you want or going out for a special dinner. Alternatively, find someone whom you respect to track your progress and provide compliments when deserved.

Managing Stressful Times

The following behavioral strategies, some of which are inspired by the E. H. Porter's writing on psychology and organizational systems theory, can help when you are overwhelmed by incoming events and experiencing distress:

Filtering is a way of determining what's most important and attending to it. Trying to attend to everything at once is a recipe for disaster. It often pays to ignore less important demands and give your attention to those that are most significant.

Queuing is putting an order to events in a way that confirms priorities for action. Obviously, the most important ones should be addressed first. Yet, sometimes you'll have several small items to handle that simply require a phone call or some small action to get them out of the way. By taking such actions, you can lower your distress by giving yourself the feeling that you have accomplished something. *Doing* is more helpful than *stewing*.

Organizing is helpful to get all your resources together and plan an approach. Sometimes several different issues can be handled with one approach. Facing a lot of problems, you may find that they can be grouped into those involving finances, those involving health, those involving future decisions versus those that are immediate, those that need to be scheduled, etc. Thinking before you leap can help avoid taking a path that only leads to even more disastrous consequences, thereby increasing your distress level.

Load sharing is finding help to handle the situation. In a good relationship, your partner can be a major strength. In a family emergency, adult children can be invited to contribute, and sometimes even young ones may have something to offer. It can also be a good way to have your action proposals assessed for their value in resolving your distress.

Get consulting help from others who have had experience dealing with distress and can give you advice and expertise. Remember, you don't have to handle everything yourself. Sometimes discussion groups of those with similar problems can help provide insights and techniques to help you cope with your situation.

Don't respond immediately to a distressing situation until you feel you can handle it. You will find you don't always have to respond *right now*. This is not easy for those who feel they need to handle everything life throws at them immediately, but it is a necessary skill to develop for healthy responses to stress.

Check your perceptions to find that perhaps the threat you felt wasn't really a threat at all. Perhaps a remark that you thought was insulting was merely an offer to help. If you're unsure, think positively and check your perceptions by asking the person who spoke or appeared to threaten you.

Search for alternatives by asking, just when you're at your wit's end, *What other possibilities can be useful here?* As an illustration, consider the case of a man who lost his managerial post, had a home that was about to be repossessed, and was unable to see where he could get funds for keeping his family alive, when he discovered relatives and friends were willing to help. He swallowed his pride, acknowledged his disastrous state of affairs, and started working as a handyman. Within four years, he had established and grown a new business, employing over 20 people.

Sharing feelings of distress. Sometimes talking about the distress is a valuable coping step and lowers tension. Here is a statement from one woman stricken with breast cancer: "I was completely depressed when I learned I had cancer, feeling my life was at an end. When I joined a survivor's group, I learned there were lots of opportunities for a positive outcome, and even if there weren't, there were still ways to improve things for me and those I loved."

Meditating for relaxation and insight. Dr. Dean Ornish, leading heart doctor to President Clinton and author of several best-selling books on the subject, believes that everyone can benefit from the practice of meditation. If you want to learn more about meditation, see the reference section in the Appendix of this book. It's a good idea to make some kind of meditation a part of your life.

As you read the list above, we hope it occurs to you that there are almost an infinite number of ways to cope—you simply have to keep open to the possibilities. Don't narrow your thoughts to only one choice—that will only add to your distress if it isn't the right one. As a friend who was an expert chess player once said, "Life is a chess game. Before you move any piece, know all the options that are open to you and the costs for making a wrong move." We couldn't agree more.

Finally, life isn't easy, but full of ups and downs. Take advantage of all the help you can get and be good to yourself! Enjoy life, explore the many possibilities available to you, and try out some new ones!

Summary

- Know how you respond to distress and be alert when you are reacting in predictable ways.
- See if you can identify the source of your distress.

- Check to see if your interpretation is correct.
- Realize you don't have to respond to a crisis right at the moment, except when facing a real emergency.
- Realize you don't have to face the distress alone. You can get help.
- Review the techniques for coping and use them as appropriate.
- Accept some distress as part of your living experience and realize there are always many possibilities for dealing with it.

Chapter 9
Making Change Happen

If you're like most people, you look forward to relationships with your spouse and family improving, your financial security increasing, more meaningful work experiences in your career, and better health. Yet despite the favorable prospects, it is difficult at times to implement the change to bring these goals into reality. At other times, you may find it easier to make changes happen than you had imagined it would be.

In this final chapter, we will look at the reasons why change is so problematic and how you can overcome obstacles to bring about desired changes. Throughout this book, we have been exploring possibilities for happiness in five key areas of life and offering ways to deal with the distress you may encounter. Now we will explore how you can bring about the changes you want to see happen, both in your own life and in the lives of people close to you.

The Tyranny of Habit

One of the greatest obstacles to realizing change is the tyranny of habit. Much of what we do in life is automatic, consisting of actions practiced repeatedly to become habits that are hard to break. Eating habits, for example, get established over countless instances when you have eaten certain foods and avoided others. If you haven't eaten fish for many years, the thought of doing so, regardless of its health value, may not be attractive. You may turn up your nose at the very mention of trying a dish of salmon. If you're a smoker, you've lit up a cigarette so many times, you can't think of not doing it. Indeed, food preferences and smoking are two of the hardest habits to break when making a change, despite the best of intentions.

In more subtle ways, how you parent, make friendships, spend money and work are also influenced by habitual practice. It's hard to stop saying no to your children's requests if that has been your frequent and automatic response to their requests over time. Listening fully to someone in a conversation may be impossible if you are habitually concerned only about making your points. Not having a morning Starbucks coffee may feel so unpleasant that you couldn't think of foregoing it, even if you're in severe financial trouble and need to cut back on extra expenses.

Changing more complex behavior, such as showing appreciation when you are usually critical, may be even harder to achieve. Starting to exercise regularly, if you've never done it, can seem so onerous and unpleasant that you might not even begin. Being assertive when dealing with people after a lifetime of deference is hard to do. Stopping your first reaction to a situation and thinking of other possible ways to respond is something that won't occur to you when you are used to seeking an immediate "quick-fix" answer to problems.

These and many other habits can be tyrannical in your life, keeping you stuck in old patterns of undesired behaviors and preventing you from living new possibilities. Changing these behaviors begins with looking at what stops you—those underlying, fundamental deterrents to change.

Basic Deterrents to Change

If you have been inspired to make changes in your life and are ready to break some old habits for new possibilities, the first step is to examine what it is that has been stopping you. Following are several deterrents to change for you to be aware of, each with helpful alternatives suggested, so you can make progress towards new possibilities in every area of your life.

Lack of Planning and Measurement. Because habits are hard to break, a major cause of failure in changing an old habit is a lack of planning. Without a plan, it's all too easy to fall back into your old ways and not find the time to do the things you must do to bring about the change you want.

Concerned about his health, Irv manages to devote 45 minutes each day to jogging, a practice he has maintained for many years. Allan, who knew he could benefit from a similar practice, never did any exercise until after he underwent a quadruple by-pass heart operation. Now he has a plan of going to a gym three days a week for special cardiovascular exercises. In addition to his regular exercise schedule, he measures his blood sugar levels regularly and watches his diet carefully, getting on the scale and checking his weight daily.

When you are trying to change any behavior, it's important to regularly check your progress to make sure you're handling things properly and behaving correctly to get the results you want. Simply trying isn't enough—it also takes measuring and evaluating your efforts. If the area is fitness, you might get your performance reviewed by a personal trainer, refer to and updating records and checklists, or sign up for fitness classes that help you track your progress on a regular basis. Measurement provides accountability, and therefore helps motivation.

When designing your plan, it's important to take small steps and then expand the scope of the change after you've had time to accustom yourself to the change. This way, you gain confidence and then go on to bigger steps. Too often the desire to be better encourages you to take a larger step than you're prepared to take and the result can be defeating, because you bit off more than you can chew.

Low Self-Evaluation. If you don't think very highly about yourself, it's hard to change. A young woman we know has been overweight for many years and is very concerned about her appearance. She recently underwent a divorce and feels as if there must be something wrong with her, as if she were unlovable. In her marriage, she would accept critical comments about her weight from an abusive husband as appropriate and deserving. She blamed herself for the divorce, and although she has the best of intentions about losing weight, she hasn't initiated any plan to do so. Fortunately, however, she started working with a therapist and is now beginning to take some positive steps towards higher self-esteem and practicing new behaviors.

You must first feel good about yourself—that is, *worthy* and *deserving*—to make beneficial changes in your life. Feelings of guilt, a history of deprecating evaluations, and social adjustment problems are not promising experiences for successfully initiating change. As in the case of the young woman above, some kind of therapeutic treatment may be required to deal with psychological issues before change can get underway. Beliefs can translate into low self-regard statements, such as, *I've never been able to follow any regimen or schedule—I just can't seem to do it!* which doesn't help, so try to catch yourself and eliminate those kinds of statements.

A higher sense of deserving comes naturally when you experience an increase in your self-esteem. In financial matters, periodically saving money and making regular investments can lead to increased self-regard, as well as financial security. In work, planning changes in managerial behavior, regularly implementing them, and having them positively evaluated by your boss and colleagues can lead to improved employee relationships.

Positive self-evaluation is something you can use to help others achieve new skills. As we reported in Chapter III on intimate relationships, when you schedule time once a week to offer a positive comment to your partner and increase that practice steadily for several weeks, you improve rated satisfaction in the relationship for both of you. A similar result occurs when you plan meetings with your children to hear about their experiences, listen to their feelings, and express appreciation for their openness.

Too Much Pressure. Rebelliousness isn't only the province of teenagers. Adults also rebel, especially if they feel unappreciated and pressured to change. When you are beleaguered by constant nagging about considerate behavior, expenses, diet, weight and exercise, it can have the opposite effect of what others want to see. For some people, until they believe it is up to them to make the change and there is no outside pressure, change won't happen.

An example of this dynamic is easy to see when dealing with children. A mother, upset about her 10-year-old's refusal to keep his room tidy, finally said to him, "I'm not going to clean your room anymore. It's now completely up to you." The result is she didn't have to do any more cleaning when the son could hardly find what he needed. As a result, the appearance of the room slowly improved.

The Role of the Unconscious. Sometimes, events in your early life that still have an unconscious hold on you can influence your ability to change. In the case of our overweight friend who felt she didn't deserve to change, guilt over the past made her believe that whatever happened was her just due.

Another person might just give up, especially after a history of serious illnesses, as in the case of a friend who had severe cardiovascular problems. Feeling himself get more and more fatigued, he eventually developed fluid in his lungs and experienced missing heart beats. A defibrillator was prescribed, but he refused it, deciding he didn't want to be bothered by the constant doctor visits that would be required. Knowing that the outcome of his condition was likely to be a painless death, he chose to accept the possible consequence—a suicidal wish with deep roots of guilt from the past, limiting his sense of deserving to live. We see this same phenomena with others who in the past prided themselves on their independence and find adhering to a rigid discipline is already a kind of death. As one of our friends, a diabetic, remarked, "If I have to give up eating all the foods I like, then there's no point in living."

Fear of Change. Often when venturing into a new field of employment, making a relationship change, or undergoing a new treatment regime, people hesitate, because they are afraid about what will happen to them. With respect to changing jobs, an employee may feel unable to maintain the same level of excellence he or she had previously exhibited, be apprehensive about the time and stresses associated with the new position, or anticipate the negative impression peers may have.

This kind of fear of failure can be extremely anti-motivational. A person who was being encouraged to join a therapy group for marital problems questioned, "Okay, suppose I become more sensitive and caring, listen more carefully to my partner, and demonstrate more affection, and then all my efforts at aren't reciprocated?" A similar fear prevented a friend from changing his financial status. "If I start an investment program, what will I do if I lose money instead of increasing the principal?" he asked, objecting to making any kind of change that might pose a risk. Instead, he did nothing and lost an opportunity to change his financial situation.

Sometimes, having only partial information for making an important decision can lead to fear and inhibition. A friend refused to undergo a needed heart operation because he'd heard that the procedure was highly risky. In fact, less than 1 percent of those operated on ever suffered any serious effects! In such instances, it's important to get information from more than one source, preferably from experts.

Imagined fears of impending change thrive when full information isn't available. We see this in large companies when change is afoot and people feel their jobs are threatened. Making a comparative list of benefits and risks involved in any change can help provide a picture that allows for more informed decisions and less resistance to change. Management could minimize such resistance by providing information about how those fears will be dealt with before changes are implemented.

Low Initial Success. You may start a program for change with strong motivation, but get discouraged when the results don't show up in some tangible way. For example, you begin to diet and exercise but see nothing on the scale or in your appearance initially, and decide it isn't working. But the scale and mirror may be reflecting your unduly high expectations. Many exercises require practice before they begin to work. In addition, low levels of distress, improper sequencing, or failure to increase the practice target may all contribute to you receiving less benefit than you expected. Possibly, the activity you chose is at such a level of difficulty that you can't master it easily, causing a lot of discomfort, even pain and discouragement.

As we indicated in the previous chapter, be smart and set initial goals low to allow for achievable results in the early stages of any change program you undertake. Seeing results is one of the most motivating factors in keeping up, so give yourself an edge, whether in areas of physical fitness and health, financial improvement, relationship changes, parenting or career changes.

Lack of Positive Acknowledgment. Change requires effort and commitment, but it can also involve acknowledgment by others. If no one notices your changes, and you receive little acknowledgment and encouragement, your motivation naturally diminishes. This is especially true for those people who are more dependent upon social recognition. Even though you may be feeling better and think you look better, you may require others to notice your improvements in order to stay motivated. Check in with your partner or close friends, and let them know how you have changed. Don't brag but do inform people in your life of the results you are getting and give them the opportunity to acknowledge you for your progress.

Comparing Yourself to Others. If you happen to be in a situation where others around you are also trying to change, and you don't exhibit change as rapidly as them, you can begin to feel like a loser by comparison and stop making the effort. Especially if you begin exercising at an older age and attend a gym filled with younger people moving effortlessly and at intense paces, it's easy to feel defeated at the start.

It may help to look for a gym where there are a number of older clients. A woman we know sought out a trainer who was in her own age group and then joined a club that had a balanced representation of all age levels. She hadn't realized how discouraging it was to constantly be in the presence of younger women in much better shape than herself, and able to do many of the exercises and activities she could not do.

Key Factors to Make Change Happen

While there are many deterrents to change that can be discouraging, there are also ways you can encourage and support change, both in you and in those around you at work, in families, health matters, intimate relationships, and financial situations. The following are several key factors that you must consider if you want to make changes in your own life. Then, after that we will discuss the best ways you can bring about change in others.

Wanting To Change. First and foremost, in order to change you must want to change. Change involves effort, and too often, people are likely to feel comfortable with the way things are and not want to rock the boat. Others don't change, because they don't believe what is recommended. These are patients who see their physicians regularly but don't follow the advice they are given. Some people will say they are going to change but don't do it, because they are only concerned about being liked or following the current fad. Pain and life-threatening events often provide the missing motivation. It's surprising what a heart attack can do to make you want to watch your diet, follow up on your blood work, and get into the gym.

Commitment to Discipline. Right behind wanting to change is discipline, an essential factor in any program of change. Some people find it impossible to adhere to a schedule, whether it is a financial budget or an exercise routine. They feel to do so would be a constraint on their freedom, preferring spontaneity to order. However, change requires a commitment to discipline. Exercise isn't always anticipated with eagerness, and often you may feel like avoiding the effort and possible pain altogether. However, having discipline ensures that you do what's required.

Practicing Change. To make a particular change become real in your life, you must actively practice that change. For example, if you want to improve relationships in your life, you must practice new ways of relating to yourself and others at home, at work, and in outside relationships. Practice and then some kind of follow-up evaluation of how you're doing enables change to be realized more rapidly.

One way to practice change is to learn new things, such as keeping up to date on the latest in technology in your field to bring to bear new knowledge and increased efficiency in your work. A physician friend commented how he would only look for treatment help from someone who had recently graduated from an institution of high reputation or who'd been associated with research on new medication. "Those are the ones who bring the latest and best knowledge to the field," he told us. "Many of my colleagues haven't learned anything new and are only doing what they already know!" If you think about the rate of change going on in professional fields such as medicine, you would certainly want to keep on learning actively throughout your career.

Yes, You Can. The classic children's book, *The Little Engine That Could*, emphasizes the value of believing you can accomplish what you set out to do. A belief in your ability to change and the positive outcome goes a long way to making good things happen. Start making changes with that in mind. Indeed, professional basketball players imagine their shot going through the basket before they shoot. The image of success helps direct progress toward that goal.

Emotional Support From Others. For those who lack discipline, having a friend who shares exercise, dieting and even measuring results can make a difference in just how much change occurs. Having a partner or joining a group that regularly exercises can be an important motivational factor. This is especially valuable when such support can be provided by your intimate partner or someone with whom you can talk about common interests, making exercise a socially pleasant event.

When people around you change easily—your partner tries harder to make changes, your parents show they're doing more to show interest, the family has a habit of saving, colleagues enroll in management training programs, and friends periodically engage in mutual exercise—it becomes easier for you to change. In fact, it often helps to have a "change buddy" who schedules his/her activities with you and provides feedback about the changes that occur. Some people join a group as a way of reinforcing their change efforts, using the example of others to provide a positive stimulus.

Exercise: Consider the Alternatives

Whatever it takes to change, do it! What are the alternatives? A valuable exercise is to consider some probable alternatives to *not* changing your current habits. Answer the question for yourself: If I don't make a change in (intimate relationships, parenting, finances, work, health), and things remain exactly as they are right now, what will my life look like in the next 5 years? 10 years? 20 years?

Write down a few sentences in your journal to describe that life you will be living if nothing you do changes in a specific are of your life, and decide if that's how you want your life to go.

For example, if you are having difficulty going quickly up and down the stairs in your home, or getting in an out of your car, think of what it will be like if you continue to lose muscle mass with the years. You will probably be unable to manage the stairs in your home, or even worse, you will be hampered by some debilitating condition and become confined to a wheel chair with your freedom and movement restricted severely. Making changes now, such as joining a gym, hiring a personal trainer or committing to a daily strength training program at home, can forestall such outcomes. When you clearly see the future that awaits you without any change in it, it can be very motivating!

Changing Others

Trying to change another person is often a futile effort, despite your best intentions. You may want to help the other person because of love, concern over health, or success. Certainly, in dealing with children, this is a very active enterprise. With a partner, it may be less so. Often a partner's comments are interpreted as rejecting and critical, stimulating their defensiveness and reluctance to change.

How can your efforts be best directed? First, the person you want to help must want to change, or at least desire the benefits of change in terms of what is important to him or her. For example, you may be highly rational and want your less rational partner to be more organized and thoughtful about expenses. But being more organized may not be important to her, while being perceived as a loving person may be. In such an instance, caring behavior on your part may be more motivational than rationality or practicality.

Also, you may want to consider other possibilities than changing the person. For example, if you are organized, perhaps you can take care of some tasks and your partner can be responsible for some others. Perhaps you can afford to hire someone who can help organize the house or office, or serve as an assistant to that person. Maybe you can change the way you react to disorganization, so it doesn't bother you so much.

However, considering our discussion in the previous chapter, habits can be so entrenched that even though you may exert a lot of pressure, there is no change. You might be better off simply accepting the person as he or she is. Allan's father used to say, "Everybody is a little crazy. Don't make the mistake of believing they can give it up." The more you criticize and provide pressure, the more the response is likely to be resistance rather than compliance, so you're constantly involved in counter-productive behavior. It's also important to have patience and remember that it took the other person years to get the way they are, so don't expect that you'll suddenly notice an overnight difference.

Sometimes an open expression of concern can bring about an unexpected change. Parents dealing with a misbehaving child who almost drove them crazy, were surprised when talking with his brother to learn that the "wild one" felt his parents didn't love him. When the parents started providing more personal time and affection, much of the crazy behavior ceased.

You can't change everything, so you must decide on what's important and what is not. For example, urging someone to put down the toilet seat down may not be as important as supporting someone to take better care of their health.

We refer back to our first key factor in making change happen, that a person has to want to change. Understanding this, you may want to discuss with the person you want to change how they see you as being helpful to them in the process, as well as offer options for how you can contribute to them. They may suggest you raise a hand when you see them exhibiting the undesired behavior, but not say a word. Go along with their suggestion, even if you don't agree that what they want is best. What is important is that you are respecting their desire to change, not imposing your own desire onto them and causing them to rebel.

To emphasize the point again: make sure you provide recognition and acknowledgement of changes in a positive manner, so the other person feels it is worthwhile to change. Too often, the person desiring change is all too prone to saying, *There you go again—You'll never change!* reinforcing a defeatist attitude on the part of the person they want to change.

Offer a trade by saying, "If you do what's important for me, I'll do something that's important to you." One might, for example, ask a child to clean up his room and offer to provide some special time with him or her. If an employee files reports on time, then you might reward them by making less demands or not doing something that irritates that other person.

If dealing with a more complex behavior, you can offer to provide help or coaching in an encouraging way that will help the other person to experience success in the process, sometimes by example, sometimes by explanations, and even by outside help. A good coach doesn't do everything for the trainee but allows the person to take on as much as can be handled independently, adding additional requirements gradually. Don't expect immediate success and change when dealing with entrenched habits. You can't try to stop someone from worrying about expenses and then expect to see a change overnight! It doesn't matter that they have more money than they will ever need. In some instances, you may be dealing with deeply unconscious fears that require therapeutic help.

Knowing someone isn't going to change, because they haven't shown any change in many years, what is the best thing to do? If you're concerned and loving, you'll have to take on changing yourself and be prepared to take care of what the other person can't, working around the difficulties presented by their behavior and attitudes. In the case of the financially anxious person, you may have to step in and say, *I'll take responsibility for the outlay that's required,* or provide constant reassurance and demonstrate mathematically that the expense can be readily afforded. Granted, such repetition may be annoying, but it clearly beats assuming that the other person is going to change and then suffer repeated disappointment. The alternative, if this is so terribly frustrating, is to turn a "deaf ear" when negative comments are made, and go ahead with other things. Possibly, you may have to terminate the relationship as a last chance solution.

Changing Your Relationship

In intimate relationships, you can fall into many traps when you attempt to make changes. Be careful not to get locked into contests where one or the other wants (or needs) to win an argument, regardless of the cost. If either one is so driven by winning, then the relationship is going to be shortly in jeopardy. Even if you or your partner win most of the time, the loser will consciously or unconsciously try to get back at the winner, meaning no one really wins.

It is important for you both to value the marriage itself and be willing to guard against anything that might threaten or destroy it. This same dynamic also applies to work situations where one colleague is arguing with another. Unnecessary conflict can persists and get out of hand, when solving the problem is not of paramount interest compared to the ego gratification of winning.

In Chapter III, we recommended dialogues for couples to use in handling differences, rather than arguments. A dialogue is a discussion to understand each other's views and reasons, while an argument is an attempt to defeat the other's point of view and ignore his or her feelings. In arguments, problem-solving becomes secondary and ceases to exist. When one wins, the other loses, and so does the relationship. In emotionally healthy marriages, needless to say, dialogue outweighs argument. Open dialogues that are geared to solving problems enhance relationships and often lead to growth and change, providing there is interest in understanding the other person, even though he or she may hold a different belief or conviction.

Reducing Resistance to Change

Changing people is easier when you take steps to reduce their resistance to change. The following is an example of how a corporation dealt positively with employees when it instituted a major change in how business would be done.

A corporation decided to terminate a large division, an event which was recognized as being potentially threatening to employees. To minimize the resistance and fear, the CEO brought all the employees together, described what was going to happen, and provided six month's warning about the change. Everyone was assured that they could obtain a position within the corporation at other locations and provided with a moving bonus should they accept that offer. The company also arranged to have seminars offered for employees who decided to look for positions elsewhere, providing help in writing resumes, assistance from recruiters, and even therapeutic discussions for those seriously impacted by the change. Since the business required continued production, those people who stayed until the end received a bonus in addition to their salaries. All employees received a termination bonus of one month's salary for each year of employment.

In more personal matters, you can reduce resistance to change by setting an example. As parents, when you show your children that you are making a habit of periodically changing—for example, switching chores, changing grocery stores, re-decorating rooms—it makes it easier for them to embrace change. This is especially true if you can show them it can be fun and rewarding to change.

It's also important to not forget to compliment children when they have changed or are changing. Similarly, if you're a business manager, it helps to demonstrate to employees your commitment to changing ineffective and undesirable behavior by changing your own behavior first. Then they will be more motivated to demonstrate such change themselves.

Listening is More Than Hearing

One of the most powerful tools for change and improving relationships is *listening*. In Chapter III on intimate relationships, we stressed the importance of really hearing what is said. Listening requires more than just hearing. It also requires an active stance to receiving the words and meaning of another person, something that is not as easy as you might think.

Signs of Listening Actively

How often have you heard the comment that you weren't listening when you thought you were? Or you thought you heard another person but missed what was behind the words that were being said? *Listening actively* means you pay fully attention to the other person.

When you are actively listening to another person, you are:

- Not doing anything else.
- Facing the person and looking at him or her.
- Not thinking of anything except what the other person is saying.
- Providing feedback to show you understood the person and checking to see if your response was accurate.

In the article, *What Understanding and Acceptance Means to Me*, the well-known psychologist Carl Rogers wrote that when he listened to another person and accepted what was being said, something interesting happened: he began to change and so did the other person.

This kind of listening Rogers is talking about means hearing not only the words but the tones, intonations, things not said, and the feelings behind the words. For example, a person might say, "I thought that wasn't bad," in response to reading something you'd written, actually meaning it was awful. This would make quite a difference if you misunderstood the person to like what you'd written. By responding, "Sounds like you felt it wasn't really up to what you expected," you could verify the person's reaction and then have a discussion about what he or she disliked.

By listening with *acceptance*, we mean that you understand what was important to the other person and not judge it or defend yourself against what is being said. It's surprising what happens when you listen this way. For example, if you haven't been listening to your child with acceptance and then you do, you'll probably notice he or she will look at you in a surprised manner and then nod in agreement, possibly continuing to talk more about an area of concern.

If you want to dialogue with another person, then it is imperative to learn to listen actively with acceptance. Otherwise, there is no opportunity for an exchange that will allow either or both of you to change your thinking. Listening actively also shows respect. If you haven't heard the other person and simply go on to state your own ideas, then your partner, child or colleague may feel somewhat rejected, as if you didn't believe what they had to say was important. If this is characteristic of your interactions, then over time the other person will begin to feel disrespected and resentful. A relationship becomes closer when each of you feels the other person is fully interested in what you have to say. It grows even more when you address your remarks to the other person's concerns before you differ with them.

If someone is angry, first acknowledge their anger and then try to find out why they feel that way. Don't start to defend before you understand. This isn't easy! It may help to try to formulate your listening response in the following way: "You feel (name the feeling) about (state the content)."

In the example mentioned above about showing someone your writing, this would be: "You felt disappointed that my writing didn't meet your standards?" The question mark is inserted to remind you that your response is questioning the speaker about the accuracy of what was said. At first, such a way of responding may seem artificial, but as you practice and gain experience, you'll become more facile, and the conversation will flow more readily. By phrasing your statements in a questioning mode, you can avoid the danger of "mind-reading." Remember it's always the speaker who is the ultimate judge of the accuracy of any interpretation.

When you begin doing more active listening with a partner or colleague, you might discover that neither of you has been fully listening to each other. Most of the time, we only hear with half an ear. Not every conversation needs your full attention, but when important matters are at stake, active listening is critical and can make a huge difference in the quality of the relationship.

Measuring Your Change – An Ultimate Score

You have probably gained some new insights while reading this book and hopefully know more now than when you began. For us, looking back has been a valuable experience, and we hope that our hindsight has become your foresight, bringing you new possibilities for increasing your happiness in life.

Make a rating of the difference these new insights could make in your life on a scale of 1-10, with 10 being the maximum possible rating for happiness in that area of your life. Place those ratings in the blanks to the left of each item below, for both your current status (Current Rating) and for the status that reflects your future improvements (Improved Rating) over a period of one year. This will give you an idea of the amount of change you want to make over the next year to bring about the happiness in your life you now know you can have!

Measuring Change

Current Rating	Improved Rating
_____Intimate Relations	_____Intimate Relations
_____Parenting	_____Parenting
_____Financial Security	_____Financial Security
_____Work	_____Work
_____Health	_____Health
_____Stress	_____Stress
_____Change	_____Change

Total Points: _____   **Total Points:** _____

Take this measurement every year, rating current happiness and showing improvements you want to see. Have your partner rate you as well. Then compare your ratings with those of your partner, or others, and have a discussion about your ratings. Examine the reasons for any change or lack of it, and the possible changes that could improve the scores. Such accountability and evaluation will help to motivate you and keep new, good habits more firmly in your life.

And most important, always enjoy seeking out new possibilities to solve current problems. Possibilities are abundant in every area of life, and only need to be discovered and embraced for a happier, healthier, and more fulfilling life.

Enjoy the Possibilities!

Addenda

After completing *If We Knew Then, What We Know Now*, we found that there were two important aspects of life we hadn't covered but wish to include. The first is *Ethics and Religion* (Addendum A) and pertains to Chapter 4 Parenting; the second is *Care-giving for the Elderly*, (Addendum B) and pertains to Chapter 7 Health.

A. Ethics and Religion

While many of us regard religious training as the fundamental basis for behaving ethically, it is more accurately the behavior of parents and peers that provide the cornerstone for influencing the integrity and caring of children, both positively and negatively.

As a parent, you hope your children will grow up to be ethically responsible adults. If you are religious, you hope they will become followers of your own faith and therefore benefit by the guidance available from your faith. But what is the best way to bring about that outcome?

Many possibilities exist for how to bring about your children's ethical and religious training. Among them are:

- You could do nothing and leave it all to others.
- You could provide personal guidance and advice.
- You could make sure your child has some religious education.

- You could rely on the influence of teachers and peers.

The first possibility, doing nothing, is unlikely to occur, since parents naturally provide discipline in the form of praise and blame, and then explain their reactions by reference to some moral code or belief. Examples of parental statements conveying moral beliefs are:

- *You know that it isn't right to lie!*
- *One of the most important commandments is to honor your father and mother.*
- *The disrespect you showed your mother needs punishment.*
- *Good girls don't let boys touch them anywhere.*

As for the second possibility, providing personal guidance and advice, your success will depend on the integrity of your own behavior. If you fail to behave in ways that are ethical, then your children will see that failure and are not likely to behave the same way. If you are a person of integrity and honesty, and you adhere to the behaviors espoused by your religion, then your children will see that and will be more likely to fulfill your hopes and follow a similar path.

The third possibility, putting your children's religious training in the hands of others, can be a positive choice, resulting in them having a sound foundation in the faith you follow. Relying on the influence of teachers and peers—if they are of your own religion—can accomplish the same goal. However, if you fail to educate your children about appropriate behavior and religious beliefs, they can hardly have a good basis for deciding whether to commit themselves fully to the practices that you espouse. In addition, you might want them to become familiar with and appreciate other religious views to insure they gain acceptance and understanding of perspectives that differ from their own.

Bottom line, the behavior you want to see in your children requires some demonstration of consistency on your own behalf. You are the most important model for your child, although fortunately, not the only one available. Think about what you enjoy and how you feel about participating in your faith's rites, holidays and customs. Do you express that joy, assuring that your children too have joyous experiences and satisfaction? Or do you simply expect your children to engage in the activity out of a sense of obligation and duty, which is hardly the best motivation.

Certainly some teachers, relatives and friends can also be powerful influences, but as a parent, it's necessary for you to evaluate your own ethical behavior and discover any discrepancies in what you are advocating for your children. Then you can provide explanations that make sense and even demonstrably change your behavior. Without any evaluation of your own behavior, you run the risk of displaying a hypocritical attitude toward the very beliefs you want your children to follow.

You can, of course, reject any child who fails to follow your footsteps, and some parents do. Indeed, members of some orthodox religions take such occasions as a cause for such grief that it is equal to the death of the child. However, another possible response is to accept the fact that your child had to evolve his or her own set of beliefs and values that made sense to him or her, and to appreciate that process as meaningful. With this view, you could support your child's choices, even though it may be personally painful to experience when those choices are different than yours.

The challenge becomes even more dramatic when a child chooses to marry someone outside of your religious group. How will you accept his or her choice? You always have many possibilities and different consequences to consider. Such decisions are not easy, for they are laden with tremendous emotional content, but the important thing is to realize you do have a choice about how you are going to respond, and that choice can affect your relationship with your child—and their children—over your and their lifetimes.

When making such choices, keep in mind that morality is an issue that tends to be heavily influenced by peers and also by the times we live in. Think of how bathing suits have changed over the years, how dormitories in many universities today are mixed, and how most married people have had prior sexual experiences. Social responsibility has also undergone many changes. Today, people use seat belts as a habit, whereas when first introduced, it took considerable pressure for everyone to follow the practice. Now, most people agree that you are endangering your own safety and that of your passengers if you don't insist on the use of seat belts in your car. All of this points to the necessity for a belief system to be flexible and up to date. If instead, you have a very rigid code, it means your children may be subject to ridicule and rejection by their friends and associates.

Regardless, you can't ever hope to control all of your children's behavior. Indeed, you shouldn't even try. Hopefully, through example, education, practice and experience, your children will internalize a guidance system that enables them to behave well, and thus attain happiness and success in their lives.

Stories of Ethical and Religious Upbringing

The following examples, taken from conversations we have had with friends and associates on this subject, show the many factors affecting religion and ethical behavior, and provide some insight into how parents can best influence their children.

One friend commented about his own experience as follows:

My father was a deeply religious Baptist and seldom failed to attend church every Sunday. He read the Bible regularly and insisted on our attending Sunday school. Yet he was a highly bigoted man with a narrow outlook, and failed to appreciate the importance of accepting and valuing diversity in a democracy. While espousing values such as honesty, he cheated on his income tax and often distorted the importance of his position at work. He was a supervisor in a corporation, but boasted about being the Director of Research—a flagrant lie. As a result, with the hypocrisy of my father's behavior in mind, I decided to have nothing to do with religion itself, but rather concerned myself with being a decent human being.

A woman commented on the value of her religious experience:

I came from a family that called itself Jewish but I never received any religious training, although we celebrated many holidays. It was later in life when a friend invited me to attend a temple where I experienced the warm acceptance of members and the spiritual beauty of prayers. I took advantage of classes to understand more about the

history, beliefs and values of the religion that were impor-
tant. Now, after ten years as a member of that same tem-
ple, I have many people whom I can count on for support
and friendship.

A 60 year-old man commented:

At an early age I was forced by my parents to
attend services whether I wanted to or not. The Catholic
school I attended was taught by sisters who were demand-
ing and mean-spirited, punishing us students severely for
minor offenses. Many questions I had about religious fig-
ures, the nature of immaculate conception, and the ascen-
sion of Jesus were never explained to my satisfaction, and
the more I learned at the university, the more I began to
regard religious beliefs as creations of men to guide and
influence communities—more myths than realities. Now,
I do not belong to any religious group, married a non-
Catholic, and did not put my own children through that
kind of experience!

A fourth friend was raised by two atheistic parents who did not affiliate with any religious group and didn't celebrate religious holidays. Growing up, other children would ask him for his religious identification, and he never knew what to answer other than, "I'm an independent." He often felt isolated and sensed rejection by friends who teased him about his not having a religion. At college, his roommate happened to be Jewish and invited him to attend services with him. Our friend decided he liked the company and the feeling of belonging and decided to become one of the reformed Jews that his roommate represented. An avid student, he tried to learn as much as he could about religion in all fields. Now, as an anthropology professor, he teaches a course entitled, "The Mind of Primitive Man," and feels proud to call himself a Jew.

Finally, a colleague commented as follows:

I was brought up as a Methodist by kindly and thoughtful parents who valued their membership in the church and had made many friends in the congregation. Values were discussed along with reasons, and punishments were clearly related to our failures to do as we should have. I was told that other people had different beliefs, but we should respect them and, if possible learn what they believed and why. There was a special class on Sundays for kids where we had lots of fun and also learned history and principles. I loved the music and singing that accompanied prayers. Today, I'm an active church member and have a rich and varied social life.

Most parents want to provide their children with some sense of what they believe that is important in shaping attitudes, beliefs and values. They also want their children to share experiences that they feel are important to them—to have the same identity, whether it be Catholic, Protestant, Jewish, Muslim, etc. Usually this means having some school experience to learn customs, traditions, values and history, as well as participation in the rituals, services and holidays associated with the religious group. Hopefully, children can find roles to perform and enjoy the experience, and can share this with others who are having similar experiences.

The problems occur when parents force religious practices on children, creating experiences that may build resentment and disenchantment with the religious experience itself. Ideally, parents should be able to communicate a sense of joy and involvement with religious life and to create similar kinds of experiences for their children. These are ways more likely to have children accept the parents' religion, identify proudly with it, and participate actively.

Openness is the best policy. A willingness to hear questions, search for answers and consider alternative possibilities may result in a loss of belief in a particular area but encourage greater involvement. Rigid insistence on the validity of what was said in the Bible, church or synagogue, as absolutely true statements can create doubt and resistance, and tends to discourage beliefs.

Many parents are in conflict about the issue of their children's attendance at services and rites or holiday celebrations of customs. Children resist going to church or synagogue, for example, and parents either apply pressure or back off. Sometimes, the parents too, may be ambivalent about the meaning, significance and logic of religious events, yet feel they ought to take a stand or risk being regarded as poor parents, neglecting such an important part of life.

This can be an even greater challenge when bright children who've received a good education ask provocative questions, argue about issues, and even indicate they question sacred tenets of the religion. How you respond to such challenges as a parent will make a tremendous difference in their relationship with you, as well as to religion.

Throughout our material on parenting, we have stressed the importance of listening empathetically, trying to understand the source of a child's questions and encouraging his or her exploration. Sometimes a survey of how different religions might provide answers to their questions is a positive way of responding to their doubts. In today's times, with the education children receive, simply repeating emphatically what you believe is not enough and may even lead to a loss of respect.

On this subject, one young man commented:

My mother was very religious, prayed constantly and believed everything she read in the Bible. When I would raise questions she couldn't answer, she'd tell me that when I grew up, I'd understand it. I realized how important her religion was to her, but her response certainly turned me off. I didn't find the priests that sharp, either. However, to minimize upset, I attended services until I went to the university where I simply avoided the whole package of religious things. I've never looked back and don't feel I've lost anything.

We all need to have some understanding of origins and causes, as well as ways of finding meaning for life. We also have basic needs for security, for beneficial outcomes, and for understanding tragedies and misfortune. A religious affiliation provides a set of rituals, practices and framework for understanding events that is shared by many people who generally are proud of their identity. However, regardless of the bonding strength of that identity, truth can never be owned by one religion only, and we believe that parents should teach children respect for the different possible ways the need for meaning in life is fulfilled.

B. Care-giving for the Elderly

In the area of health, we wanted to add some additional commentary about the importance of giving care to the elderly, both in the quality of that care and on the nature of those receiving care.

As we live longer, we are aware that more and more elderly—in one form or another, whether physically or mentally—become less able to care for themselves. While the natural tendency for many of us is to want to provide help, some people may not want that help. There have always been caregivers—children for parents, spouses for each other, and less frequently, parents for disabled children.

However, the problems facing caregivers, recipients and family members can be enormous. Despite good intentions, those who are interested in helping may also be ambivalent because of many factors, including cost, resources, the drain on their own lives, as well as the attitudes, behavior and infirmities of the elderly. We have witnessed many breakdowns in health and in the quality of life, as well as financial disasters affecting the elderly.

As a result, we have observed several factors that have to be considered when care is needed. These factors may influence the effectiveness of the efforts made to help others:

1. **Identifying who will provide the care.** Will it be an individual, a shared responsibility, paid help, or a facility or hospice?

2. **Deciding when help should be provided.** Is that point at the

first sign of mental or physical deterioration assessment, or after the affected individual is helpless and incapable of fully attending to needs?

3. **Recognizing how the recipient accepts help.** It's important to determine whether the potential recipient perceives the need for help or will reject it for many reasons. Some reasons for rejection could be believing problems can be managed by his or herself, fear of loss of independence, not wanting to be a burden on loved ones, fear that needing such help may be the first signs of death, and other possible fears.

4. **Deciding where help should be provided.** Should it be at home, the home of a family member, assisted-aid home, hospital, or elsewhere?

5. **Deciding what help should be given:** a driver, household help, a walker, a wheelchair or help needed by the bedridden.

6. **Determining who should make decisions concerning help for the recipient.** Should it be an independent agent or family member(s)? Considering a situation where several people are involved: Are they compatible or likely to fight? Can they afford the time, money and effort likely to be involved? Can they provide the kind of care required consistently? How will the care affect other intimate parties?

7. **Financial considerations.** Do the resources exist for the kind of care desired?

Stories of Elder Care Problems and Solutions

We have included several personal stories that illustrate the problems involved and solutions achieved by care-givers and their recipients:

A couple between 85 and 90. The husband has been bedridden for four years with only occasional movement in a wheelchair. The wife is frail but provides 24/7 care-giving with little outside help. When viewed from an outside perspective, there could be 24/7 help for the wife to ease the strain that she experiences. There is no money available for outside help and no children. Yet the wife who makes major sacrifices in her life feels terribly guilty asking for additional help and the husband has little quality of life, if any. You can see how sad this is.

A woman in her late 70s who has dementia and physical problems that keep her wheelchair bound. Her husband has sufficient funds to place her in a nursing home, yet is torn by a promise to keep her at home. The quality of his life has been greatly diminished. He recognizes the need to place her in a nursing home yet can't make that decision. The day will come, however, when he has no choice.

Another woman in her 70s with a husband suffering from Lou Gehrig's disease. As the sole care provider, she suffered for three years at home with minimal help; then took care of him daily for two years in a board and care facility. He was unable to appreciate the care since his mental capacities were severely deteriorated. Nevertheless, although money was not an issue, she wouldn't hire additional help nor move him earlier to a hospice or other facility.

A couple in their 80s in poor physical health. The wife has had several automobile accidents yet refuses to stop driving. The dilemma is, under the circumstances, should her children force her to give up the car? In addition, the couple has done little planning for their future and are unwilling to do so now, saying, "We've always been able to manage, and we'll be able to do so for the rest of our lives!"

Knowledgeable children tried to convince their parents to move to an affordable facility. The parents refused. Shortly after, the father died. The remaining spouse is now home-bound and not eligible for the original facility, and is ailing from severe emphysema. What should the children do? The mother is very attached to her home but is increasingly unable to take care of herself. None of the children can afford the burden of providing 24/7 home care.

Children take charge. One of our friends made an attempt to direct the lifestyle of parents in need of help. However, his two siblings did not agree about such assistance, to the detriment of the parents. The siblings disliked each other and were jealous about their inheritance, which further isolated the parents.

Parents moving in with a grown child and family. An attorney has parents whom he loves very much and since they were elderly and needed assistance, he invited them to live with him and his family. The parents accepted the change at first but then became increasingly bitter and complained about many little things. Despite the family's heroic efforts to make them feel at home, they seldom complimented the wife for her cooking or expressed any appreciation for the help they received. The attorney's spouse has become extremely irritated by their behavior and wishes her husband would support her in finding another place for them to live. What can the husband do?

In the last instance, it is clear that you have to recognize how care-recipients will behave in new circumstances. It is hard for caring and supportive people to feel their efforts are not appreciated. As we grow older and require care, we also need to remember we are affecting the lives of the caregivers, and to be grateful and as pleasant as possible to reward them for their assistance in making us feel comfortable.

Resources and Solutions

What kind of help is available? Here are a few forms of help to consider:

- Support groups
- Financial assistance (private and government agencies)
- Family and friends
- Agencies that can provide advice and help (see the list provided at end of this section)

What are some preventive possibilities for better results? Consider the following:

- Advance planning, started as soon as possible when disabilities become apparent.
- Bringing family and possible caregivers together at an early stage to see how they are received, and to discuss details of care and financial responsibility.
- Preparing financially: obtaining long term insurance.
- Reconstructing a home to make things easier for elderly people (e.g., providing grab bars, lowering counters if a person is restricted to a wheel chair, etc.)

- Taking maximum advantage of professional and other knowledgeable help.
- Participating in support groups, both for the elderly and care-givers.
- Taking care of yourself if you're a potential or actual caregiver. If you become ill or incapacitated, there may be no one left to help anyone. Pay attention to your feelings – if you can't handle the burden find some way to relieve it by taking vacations, trading time with others, having a chance to discuss feelings with others, or learning how to set limits with recipients.
- Being prepared for the worst contingency but planning for the best result.

Care Giving Agencies

The following organizations can be resources for caregivers:

Family Caregiver Alliance

National Center on Caregiving
180 Montgomery Street, Suite 900
San Francisco, CA 94104
(415) 434-3388, (800) 445-1806
Email: info@caregiver.org
Website: www.caregiver.org

National Care Giving Association

10400 Connecticut Ave., Suite 500

Kensington, MD 20895-3650

(301) 942-6430, (800) 896-3650

Email: info@thefamilycaregiver.org

Website: www.afcacares.org

The Caregiver Resource Center

PO Box 122

Cos Cob, CT 06807-0122

(203) 861-9833

Email: care4you@optonline.net

Web Site: www.caregiverresourcecenter.com

Bibliography

Albion, M. *Tuesdays With Morrie.* Random House, New York, 1997

Atkins, S. *The Name of Your Game.* Ellis and Stuart, Beverly Hills, 1981

Bach, G. & Wyden, P. *The Intimate Enemy: How to Fight Fair in Love and Marriage.* William R. Murrow, New York, 1983

Cramer, J. J. *Real Money.* Simon & Schuster, New York, 2005

Drucker, P. *The Practice of Management.* Harper and Brother Publishers, New York, 1955

Frost, R. *Mountain Interval.* Henry Holt, New York, 1920

Gordon, W. J. J. *Synectics.* Harper Brothers, New York, 1961

Iscoe, I. and Stevenson, H.W. *Personality Development in Children: Papers by Harold E. Jones.* U. of Texas Press, Austin, 1960

Katcher, A. *La Importância de Ser Você Mesmo.* Editora Atlas, Sao Paulo, 1989

Katcher, A. "Applying the LIFO Method to Organizational Effectiveness," *Industrial Training International.* London. 11: 138-141.

Katcher, A. & Czichos, R. *Learning Dynamics.* X-Libris, Philadelphia, 2009

Liebman, J. L. *Peace of Mind: Insights on Human Nature That Can Change Your Life.* Citadel Press, New York, 1946

Newmark, G. *How to Raise Emotionally Healthy Children.* NMI Publishers, Tarzana, CA, 2008

Newmark, G. & Newmark, I. S. *Happiness Through Superficiality.* NMI Publishers, Tarzana, CA, 1991

Ornish, D. *The Spectrum.* Ballentine Books, New York, 2007

Piper, W. *The Little Engine That Could.* Platt & Monk, New York, 1976

Rogers, C. *Counseling and Psychotherapy.* Houghton Mifflin, New York, 1992

Roth, P. *Portnoy's Complaint.* Random House, New York, 1967

Selye, H. *The Stress of Life.* McGraw-Hill, New York, 1956

Tal Ben-Sahar. *Happier: Learn the Secrets to Daily Joy and Lasting Fulfillment.* McGraw-Hill, Boston, 2007

Vogel, S. J. & Rosin, M. *Your Mind Is Not Your Best Friend. A Guide for How Not to Get in Your Own Way.* Fresh River Press, Los Angeles, 2010

About the Authors

DR. ALLAN KATCHER has been a consultant to many of the Fortune 500 companies, including Cisco, Citibank, Exxon, General Foods, Household International, National Westminster Bank, and Xerox. He has lectured and conducted seminars in more than 20 countries. His doctorate in psychology was earned at the University of California (Berkeley), and he has taught at Brooklyn College, the California Institute of Technology, UCLA, and the University of Washington.

The former president of BCon-LIFO International, Inc., Dr. Katcher is the author of books in both Portuguese and English, and has written many articles on the LIFO Method and a variety of applications. His major interests are in executive coaching, managing change, self-concepts, and teambuilding. Prior to work on the LIFO Method, he was manager of executive development at Douglas Aircraft Company, head of management development at the System Development Corporation, and a human factors scientist at the RAND Corporation.

DR. IRVING NEWMARK is the founder of Studio City Dental Group, the longest-running dental group practice in the United States. He received his DDS from Indiana University, as well as an MA in psychology from California State University, Northridge.

Dr. Newmark is a unique combination of dentist, psychologist, and management consultant. He has been at the forefront of developing innovative methods for practice management, health care delivery systems, and improvement of the quality of doctor-patient relations.

Dr. Newmark has published extensively in professional journals. He also co-authored a book with his brother Gerald Newmark, a PhD in educational psychology, on happiness (*Happiness Through Superficiality*, 1991) and has lectured widely throughout the United States. He has been a consultant to professional partnerships and groups with respect to team building and interpersonal relationships. He has a special interest in life coaching for couples and individuals.

8472922R0

Made in the USA
Charleston, SC
13 June 2011